THE BIRTH OF
ART DECO

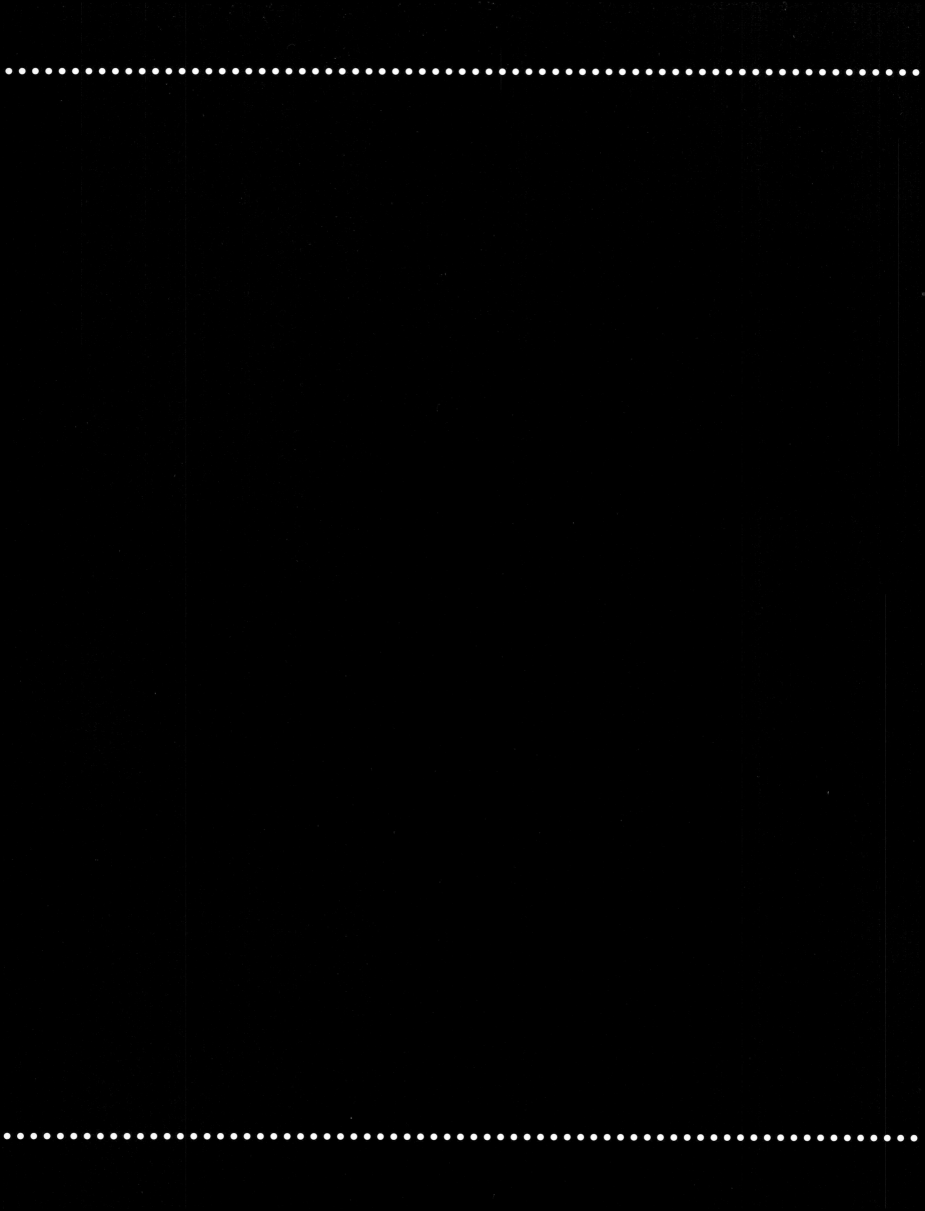

JARED GOSS

THE BIRTH OF
ART DECO

✢

*Ruhlmann and
the Hôtel du Collectionneur,
1925*

*RIZZOLI*Electa

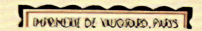

Contents

Preface 9

✛

I. French Art Deco: An Overview 10

✛

II. The 1925 Paris Exposition 26

✛

III. E. J. Ruhlmann and Pierre Patout 50

✛

IV. The Collector's House, 1925 70

✛

L'Hôtel du Collectionneur 89

✛

L'Hôtel du Collectionneur translation 137

✛

Acknowledgments 142

Preface

Twenty years ago, as a curator at The Metropolitan Museum of Art in New York, I had the pleasure of collaborating with a group of venerable colleagues on the North American presentation of *Ruhlmann: Genius of Art Deco*. The exhibition originated in France, where in 2001 it was mounted by Emmanuel Bréon at Le Musée des Années 30 in Boulogne-Billancourt. There, it was visited by curator Rosalind Pepall of the Montreal Museum of Fine Arts, who decided it would be of interest in Canada. As Bréon and Pepall shaped their traveling version of the exhibition, they approached the late J. Stewart Johnson and me at the Metropolitan for our help with loans, as the Metropolitan's collection includes important works by the French designer E. J. Ruhlmann and his contemporaries. Not only were we delighted to help, but we also agreed to host the show. An augmented exhibition was thus presented in 2004 at both the Metropolitan and in Montreal.

A catalogue accompanied the exhibition; among my contributions was an essay on the Hôtel du Collectionneur, the "Collector's House," Ruhlmann's pavilion at the Exposition Internationale des Arts Décoratifs et Industriels Modernes held in Paris in 1925. (The French term *hôtel* refers to a grand city house.) In 2014, I wrote a collection catalogue for the Metropolitan titled *French Art Deco* that examined in detail nearly one hundred works from the museum's holdings, including those by Ruhlmann and other designers, many of which had been displayed in the Hôtel du Collectionneur. My interest in Ruhlmann and his work had only grown. *The Birth of Art Deco* draws heavily on those two publications, which are foundational to the scholarship of this work.

More than a decade has passed, and the year 2025 marks the centenary of the Exposition. To honor it, a book on Ruhlmann—including a facsimile of *L'Hôtel du Collectionneur*, the beautiful record of the pavilion published by Éditions Albert Lévy in 1926—seems apropos since his pavilion represents the birth of French Art Deco.

French Art Deco, as much backward-looking as forward-looking, continues to offer a model on how to be modern within the parameters of tradition. Instead of mining the past for romanticized historicism or pastiche, French Art Deco designers encouraged something different: in the words of Louis Süe and André Mare, "The thing to do is to go back in history and start all over again;"[1] Francis Jourdain commented, "One should not lose sight of the fact that antique furniture when new was nothing else than modern furniture;"[2] and Paul Poiret stated, "It is only in being modern that we create a past for the future—that is, if we are worth anything. Even the old masters were once daring innovators."[3] As Art Deco furnishings officially become antiques, these are its lessons.

The Hôtel du Collectionneur is a model for these lessons. The fireback in its dining room presented a quotation from Racine's play *Les Plaideurs* (*The Litigants*): "Qui veut voyager loin ménage sa monture; buvez, mangez, dormez, et faisons feu qui dure." "Whoever wants to travel far takes care of his horse; drink, eat, sleep, and let's make a fire that lasts." Ruhlmann's pavilion—though it existed only for six months—is a fire that lasts.

Jared Goss

Grand salon in the Hôtel du Collectionneur, 1925 Exposition.

French Art Deco

An Overview

Art Deco was formally introduced to the world at the 1925 Exposition Internationale des Arts Décoratifs et Industriels Modernes (International Exposition of Modern Decorative and Industrial Arts) in Paris. More than 130 pavilions—mostly French, but a significant number of international ones as well—showcased the movement's expression of youthful modernity at its most exuberant, refined, and accomplished. No pavilion embodied this spirit better than Ruhlmann's.[4]

But what, exactly, is Art Deco? Among art history's most ambiguous and imprecise terms, Art Deco is today commonly (if indiscriminately) used to describe the decorative arts, architecture, and even fine arts produced internationally between the First and Second World Wars. While it is often referred to as a style, in fact there never was a single, unified Art Deco style. Art Deco's many and varied aesthetic expressions came to be as wide-ranging as the places and times where it appeared. To wit: *Art Deco* has been used to describe everything from precious Cartier jewels of ancient inspiration made in Paris during the 1910s to futuristic outboard motors made for the American retailer Sears in the 1930s—polar opposites in every way. Given this paradox, perhaps *idiom*, *taste*, or *sensibility* more accurately describes this global phenomenon.

ABOVE: Egyptian-style pendant, Cartier Paris, 1913. Platinum, diamonds, onyx, millegrain setting, and black silk cord.
OPPOSITE: *Waterwitch* Outboard Motor, 1936. Designed by John R. Morgan and manufactured by Sears, Roebuck and Company. Steel, aluminum, and rubber.

The design of this precious jewel evokes ancient Egyptian hieroglyphs (its pylon-shaped frame encloses a vase holding papyrus stalks) while the futuristic yet functional outboard motor's styling suggests a Flash Gordon spaceship.
These objects exemplify the contradictory characteristics of Art Deco, which is at once backward- and forward-looking.

Le Champagne, bas-relief plaque displayed at the 1924 Salon d'Automne. Designed and sculpted by Georges Saupique.

Indeed, the moniker *Art Deco* did not exist in its own time. Different names emerged in different places, such as *Art Moderne* in the English-speaking world and *Style Moderne* in the French. The period has been dubbed the Roaring '20s, the Jazz Age, *Les Années Folles* (the Crazy Years). The period introduced numerous romantic characters: the flapper, the vamp, and the *garçonne*; the bootlegger, the gangster, and his moll. Their background—comprising colorful locales such as nightclubs, speakeasies, and penthouse apartments—was juxtaposed by the dynamic movement of trains, ocean liners, airplanes, and automobiles.

The era also witnessed the Great Depression, the dawn of communism, and the rise of fascism. It was a period bracketed by devastating world wars. Art Deco reflects all of that: it is as varied and contradictory as its time.

But in the end, Art Deco is less about dates, activities, and personalities than it is about *things*. Art Deco isn't so much the flapper sitting in a café, enjoying a smoke and a drink while powdering her face; rather, it's her Bakelite cigarette holder, her jeweled vanity case, the chrome shaker holding her cocktail, and the

Le Café, bas-relief plaque displayed at the 1924 Salon d'Automne. Designed and sculpted by Georges Saupique.

very café itself. Art Deco is embodied in products—some luxurious, others humble—that brought glamour, elegance, sophistication, excitement, and modernity to consumers around the world. Art Deco appears not only in every aspect of the designed environment—buildings, interiors, household furnishings, and gardens—but also in personal accouterments like clothing, jewelry, and other fashionable trappings.

The term *Art Deco*—an abbreviation of the French *arts décoratifs* (itself a French shorthand for the Exposition Internationale des Arts Décoratifs et Industriels Modernes)—was coined only in the 1960s, when scholars and academics looked back on the period with the objectivity that comes with time. They recognized that the definitive moment of Art Deco coincided with the 1925 Exposition, thereby acknowledging its threefold importance: it marked the occasion when Art Deco was formally introduced, it established France as the birthplace of Art Deco, and it gave a name to the phenomenon of Art Deco. Although efforts to create a design language and products suited to modern needs and tastes took form in many places during the first decades of the twentieth century, in France they crystallized into something coherent, identifiable, and fully developed at the Exposition.

The origins of Art Deco date to the turn of the twentieth century, when many in the French design community began debating how to reinvigorate a moribund industry. Designers, museum professionals, and academics argued that during the second half of the nineteenth century a turn toward industrial production had undermined the quality of French goods. To fully understand the severity of this decline, they claimed, one need only compare modern design with that of the ancien régime, the political and social system in France before the revolution of 1789.

During the seventeenth and eighteenth centuries, France developed an international reputation for its luxury trades—producing architecture, furnishings and other decorative arts, not to mention clothing, jewelry, and perfumes, as well as wines and cuisine—of unsurpassed refinement and elegance. Métiers were taught to generations of craftsmen through the time-honored traditions of apprenticeship and guild training. French expertise in *les arts de vivre*, the arts of living, brought both prestige and economic benefits to the country and established Paris as a tastemaking capital.

The revolution abolished guilds in France, and by the end of the reign of King Louis Philippe, in 1848, most guild-trained craftsmen had either died or stopped working. The demise of artisan trades coincided with the rise of the Industrial Revolution; handcraftsmanship was replaced by machine production and work-for-hire industrial designers with little experience as craftsmen. Moreover, the rise of the middle class—many of whom had no direct knowledge of handmade objects—was believed to have lowered standards of connoisseurship: without high-quality points of reference, affordable machine-made products were considered satisfactory. In the absence of skilled artisans and discriminating consumers, who together might have advanced taste, manufacturers simply began reproducing old models using new technologies rather than developing new models that reflected their machine production, resulting in an epidemic of pastiche.

Subsequently, the early twentieth century witnessed the commercial failure of Art Nouveau, a design movement that arguably reached its peak in France at the 1900 Exposition Universelle. Few Art Nouveau designers were themselves craftsmen, and their work was criticized for its art-for-art's-sake approach. Mass production of poor-quality objects hastened its demise. A disillusioned French design community encouraged its members to learn from the mistake of insisting on artistry at the expense of craftsmanship.

As the new century dawned, critics argued that this sorry state demanded a reckoning on how to recover the high standards and savoir-faire of the preindustrial era.

Boudoir-Library, 1918. Designed by E. J. Ruhlmann. Ruhlmann's earliest designs for interiors
often incorporated sofa-lined niches or low-lying daybeds abundantly piled with tasseled cushions. Opulently draped curtains,
fringed rugs, and throws contributed further to the heady and exotic effect.

The French were aware of advances being made in other countries, particularly Germany. While sensitive to any hint of German superiority following the French defeat in the Franco–Prussian War of 1870–71, which was still fresh in public memory, French designers took note. German design organizations promoted an alliance between art and industry, producing affordable, well-designed furnishings. Their aesthetically unified rooms took inspiration from the reductive elegance of the early nineteenth-century Biedermeier style, and each interior was conceived and overseen by a single master designer.

The French soon also began mining their own cultural past for aesthetic, technical, and material inspiration. Because the last generation of guild-trained artist-craftsmen had lived during the reign of Louis Philippe, contemporaneous with the Biedermeier era, French designers related their work to the tastes of that period, although some also looked to the earlier eras of Louis XV, Louis XVI, the Directoire, and the Empire. Linking modern design with tradition became central to the mission of reviving *les arts de vivre* in the twentieth century and would assign a decidedly upmarket quality to French Art Deco.

Nonetheless, many French designers were also curious about the wider world.

A taste for exoticism flourished in the early twentieth century. Interest was piqued at Colonial Expositions held in Paris in 1907 and 1931, which encouraged French designers to take advantage of resources—raw materials and a skilled workforce—that could be imported from the French colonies in Asia and Africa. This in turn led to experimentation with new materials (ivory, exotic woods), techniques (lacquering, ceramic glazes), and forms that evoked distant cultures and faraway places.

The period also witnessed an acceptance among consumers of ideas put forth by the artistic avant-garde, especially as adapted by designers and applied to luxury objects. The dynamic effects of clashing colors and patterns in Fauvist paintings appeared in textiles, wallpapers, and other surface decorations, while the abstract shapes and geometric stylizations of Cubism were used both formally and decoratively.

French Art Deco found its most representative expression in two distinct professions with roots in the past: the specialized production of artist-craftsmen and the overarching visions of ensembliers.

Artist-craftsmen were self-defined. In the manner of guild-trained professionals, their work brought together technical know-how and an informed design sensibility. They created unique handmade objects for a discerning clientele. Among the best-known artist-craftsmen of the era were Jean Dunand (known for his metalwork and lacquer), Maurice Marinot (glasswork), and Émile Lenoble (ceramics). Other names may be more familiar today, since their legacy businesses continue to operate: Cartier (jewelry), Lalique (glass), and Puiforcat (silver).

OPPOSITE, TOP: Young girl's bedroom, ca. 1920–22. Designed by E. J. Ruhlmann. This room setting, its walls hung in Ruhlmann's *Le Parc* printed-cotton textile (ca. 1920), was installed at the Ruhlmann showroom.
BOTTOM LEFT: *Vase Ruhlmann No. 3*, ca. 1927. Designed by E. J. Ruhlmann in 1926 and produced by the Manufacture Nationale de Sèvres. Glazed porcelain.
BOTTOM RIGHT: *Sarrazin* Textile, ca. 1917. Designed by E. J. Ruhlmann. Printed linen.

OVERLEAF: State bedroom, 1928. Designed by E. J. Ruhlmann for the 1928 Salon des Artistes Décorateurs.
For this room setting, Ruhlmann reused both the massive crystal chandelier and the silk wall hangings (designed by Henri Stephany) that were originally made for the grand salon of the Hôtel du Collectionneur. Photo by Thérèse Bonney.

Garden setting at the 1925 Exposition by Robert Mallet-Stevens. *Arbres Cubistes* (Cubist Trees) designed and sculpted by twin brothers Jan and Joël Martel. Because its site on the Esplanade des Invalides did not allow for the planting of real trees, this garden featured four reinforced concrete tree-shaped sculptures exemplifying the abstracted forms and fragmented shapes of Cubism.

Parallel to the artist-craftsmen were ensembliers, who instead offered clients a broad range of services, fabricating complete interiors that achieved a harmony of colors, textures, materials, and workmanship. Their creations, conceived as total works of art, encompassed not only the traditional aspects of interior design such as furniture and objects, carpets, textiles, and lighting, but also architectural features, paintings, and sculptures, on the premise that such details were integral to aesthetic unity. Among the best-known ensembliers were E. J. Ruhlmann, Süe et Mare (directed by Louis Süe and André Mare), and Martine (directed by Paul Poiret).

Ensembliers differed from today's interior decorators in that instead of composing rooms by bringing together existing objects and materials from different sources, they designed and either manufactured or commissioned everything they needed for a desired effect. In this way, they resembled historical figures such as Charles Percier and Pierre Fontaine, architect-decorators to Napoléon I. They designed not only

Bedroom, ca. 1924. Designed by Martine, the interior design business of couturier Paul Poiret. The profusion of patterns and colors illustrates the strong influence of Fauvist painting on interior design.

houses, but also everything that went into them—down to the doorknobs—so that no single element would offend the eye because it was inconsistent with the whole. Because ensembliers were rarely craftsmen themselves, they employed teams of artisans to realize their singular vision.

The way of the ensemblier precluded mass production; it was a custom trade. Its business model was that of the couturier who designed limited quantities of clothing to sell at high prices, a fact that Ruhlmann recognized when he pointed out that "style doesn't come from the bottom. It appears in the house of the *grand couturier* and is only later taken up by the ready-to-wear trade."[5] This prescient observation was borne out when the four large Paris department stores—Printemps, Bon Marché, Galeries Lafayette, and Grands Magasins du Louvre—adopted the model, each establishing its own design studio offering similar decorating services to a somewhat less affluent clientele.

Interior, 1924. Designed by Louis Süe and André Mare. Süe et Mare, as their ensemblier business was known, was among the most celebrated French interior design firms of the 1920s. Harmonious combinations of color, pattern, and design characterize their expensive, custom-made interiors.

By the time of the First World War (1914–18), the principal characteristics of French Art Deco were established: a Janus-like expression of modernity and tradition, and an alliance of art and craftsmanship. From the start, French Art Deco was aimed at an affluent clientele that appreciated the qualities that made such modern objects equivalent to masterpieces from the past.

The war was devastating. Beyond requiring all able-bodied men to serve, materials and other resources were requisitioned for the military and non-essential production came to a halt. Only after the 1918 armistice and demobilization could France again turn its efforts to reinvigorating its design industry. Much of that activity would be focused on preparations for the forthcoming exposition. Originally planned for 1915, it was delayed until 1925 because of the war.

The city offered an array of commercial establishments selling Art Deco, many in shopping areas on the Right Bank. Ensemblier showrooms—such as those of Ruhlmann (in the Rue de Lisbonne), Süe et Mare (in the Rue du Faubourg-Saint-Honoré), and Martine (in the Rondpoint-des-Champs-Élysées)—displayed fully

Staircase in the Martine showroom, Paris, ca. 1924. The showroom was set up not only to suggest a real house but also to function as a shop selling a full range of household furnishings.

furnished interiors representing the range of what they could produce. Some artist-craftsmen businesses, such as Puiforcat and Sèvres, had dedicated showrooms as well.

Museums, such as the Musée des Arts Décoratifs, the Musée du Luxembourg, and the Musée Galliera, mounted exhibitions of modern decorative arts. Monographic exhibitions were rare, although the Lalique exhibition of 1933 and the Ruhlmann retrospective of 1934 were important exceptions. In 1937, the first survey of French Art Deco was organized by the Musée des Arts Décoratifs: *Le Décor de La Vie de 1900 à 1925*.

The Société des Artistes Décorateurs, an association for craftsmen and designers founded in 1900, presented annual Salon-style exhibitions showcasing its members' recent work. These professional exhibitions were important events that fostered interdisciplinary dialogue. Their popularity led to the organization of the much larger Exposition of 1925. The Salon practice of exhibiting complete room settings established a model for the Exposition's displays.

Maisons de couture and other fashion businesses offered lessons as well. Couturiers were in tune with the latest trends, and increasingly the public looked to them as tastemakers in general. Notable was Paul Poiret, who, in addition to running an eponymous fashion house, oversaw a perfume company and an interior design studio (given the respective names "Rosine" and "Martine" after his daughters), thereby introducing the concept of "lifestyle design."

Theaters, restaurants, and bars were equally up to date—day or night, it was impossible during the inter-war years to avoid Art Deco in Paris. Myriad publications introduced Art Deco to readers, helping them understand it and identify its key figures. Journalists reviewed exhibitions, wrote profiles, and conducted interviews disseminated in magazines and trade journals, often translating their articles into different languages. Art publishers presented deluxe folios of lavish pochoir-printed color plates, not just to show vivid color schemes but, just as importantly, to elevate their books to the level of artworks themselves.

French Art Deco was marketed to both domestic and foreign consumers, establishing *les arts de vivre* as a French national brand image. Travelers en route to France often got a first taste on ocean liners before setting foot inside the country. The French government, eager to promote its national products, recognized that their liners could serve as floating advertisements. In 1912, it drew up a contract with the Compagnie Générale Transatlantique (CGT) to build four ships over the next quarter century for its most prestigious route, the North Atlantic. Three of the four were realized: the *Paris* (1921), the *Île-de-France* (1927), and the *Normandie* (1935); the advent of the Second World War halted production of the *Bretagne*.

The CGT aimed to seduce its well-heeled passengers, who paid not so much for transportation as for atmosphere, with lavish décor, good food, and fine wines, which in turn inspired purchases upon arrival in France. With a focus on the first-class traveler (the most likely shoppers), the CGT hired the best French designers of the day to outfit the ships in the latest décor. Once in Paris, printed shopping guides—such as Thérèse and Louise Bonney's 1929 *Buying Antique and Modern Furniture in Paris*, written especially for American visitors to Paris—directed passengers to the showrooms, shops, and galleries of the very makers whose works they had admired on board.

By the late 1920s, however, the spare, functional, and industrially produced furnishings of the Bauhaus design school in Germany had captured the imagination of the international design world. But most French designers (and their clientele), accustomed to luxury production, were reluctant to follow this trend and simply clothed their expensive, one-of-a-kind designs in industrial materials or employed the reductive aesthetic of modernism. Machines played little or no role in their manufacture, and they retain an inherently ornamental quality.

The worldwide economic crisis of the 1930s dealt a serious blow to the luxury trades. Art Deco, having reached its apogee at the 1925 Exposition, gradually waned. Its decorative flourishes and emphasis on rich and exotic materials seemed increasingly irrelevant against the exigencies of the Great Depression. In 1937, the French government sponsored the Exposition Internationale des Arts et Techniques dans la Vie Moderne; less ambitious than the 1925 Exposition, the fair focused on France's place in the modern world as reflected through achievements in science and technology rather than in arts and luxury trades. The 1937 Exposition in effect marked the end of the Art Deco era.

First-class Grand Salon aboard the S.S. *Normandie*. Watercolor by Josep Simont i Guillén, 1935.
Conceived overall by architects Richard Bouwens van der Boijen and Roger-Henri Expert, the Grand Salon featured reverse-painted glass wall panels by Jean Dupas, lacquered columns and doors by Jean Dunand, tall freestanding lamps by Auguste Labouret, and furniture by Jean-Maurice Rothschild, upholstered in Aubusson tapestry by Émile Gaudissard.

With the outbreak of the Second World War (1939–45), an entire way of life disappeared. Afterwards, inexpensive housing and furnishings became the priority as millions of people around the world rebuilt their lives, leading to a boom in inexpensive, mass-produced design. The elaborate households of the prewar years were replaced by informality and adaptability. By and large, the approach to furnishings as status objects disappeared; Art Deco became obsolete.

In the mid-1960s, after two decades of postwar austerity, a new generation rediscovered Art Deco. Appreciation for its inherent qualities—refined aesthetics and exquisite craftsmanship—emerged not only among connoisseurs and collectors, but also among scholars and art historians. It was at this time that the term *Art Deco* came into use, for the first postwar exhibitions devoted to the subject mounted at the Musée des Arts Décoratifs in Paris and the Minneapolis Institute of Art.[6] Since then, interest—both scholarly and popular—has only grown. Poignantly, at the centenary of the 1925 Paris Exposition, what once had been the most modern thing in the world has officially become antique.

The 1925 Exposition

During its run, from April 28 through October 25, 1925, the Exposition Internationale des Arts Décoratifs et Industriels Modernes (the International Exposition of Modern Decorative and Industrial Arts) attracted over 16 million international visitors.

Nary a trace of it remains on its fifty-five-acre site at the center of Paris—a fact underscored by the number of structures surviving from other major expositions held in Paris over the years. But what *does* remain is unique to the 1925 Exposition, a legacy at once more ephemeral yet also more enduring: its name, abridged into the term *Art Deco*, which has come to define an era.

While the aesthetic, technical, and intellectual underpinnings of French Art Deco, exemplified in works shown at the Exposition, are linked to the preindustrial past, the Exposition was nonetheless rooted in the Industrial age, which spawned large-scale public fairs where newly manufactured products were introduced.

The first of these, the Exposition des Produits de l'Industrie Française (the Exposition of French Industrial Products), was held in 1798, and ten more followed in rapid succession: 1801, 1802, 1806, 1819, 1823, 1827, 1834, 1839, 1844, and 1849. They were mounted in public spaces large enough to accommodate their temporary structures: the Champ-de-Mars, the Cour Carrée of the Louvre (the heart of the oldest part of today's museum), the Esplanades des Invalides, the Place de la Concorde, the Champs-Elysées, and the Cours-la-Reine. The expositions focused on French products, featuring displays of works made in state-owned factories: Gobelins tapestries, Sèvres porcelains, and Savonnerie carpets, as well as technical innovations such as the Jacquard loom, scenic wallpapers, and the daguerreotype camera.

ABOVE: First Exposition of French Industrial Products, mounted in the Champ-de-Mars in Paris in 1798 and presented in a building specially designed by Jean-François Chalgrin, architect of the Arc de Triomphe in Paris.

OPPOSITE: Porte d'Orsay entrance gate, 1925 Exposition. Designed by Louis-Hippolyte Boileau.

In 1851, the Great Exhibition of the Works of Industry of All Nations—effectively the first World's Fair—was held in London's Hyde Park. Its English organizers juxtaposed British products with those made in other countries. The exhibition was housed inside a vast, purpose-built, glass-and-iron pavilion known as the Crystal Palace, designed by architect-engineer Sir Joseph Paxton. The exhibition's success caused the scope and scale of Paris exhibitions to expand dramatically, evolving into Expositions Universelles that displayed works (which increasingly included scientific and engineering inventions) from around the globe.

During the second half of the nineteenth century, four such Expositions Universelles were held in Paris: in 1855, 1867, 1878, and 1889 (the last commemorating the centenary of the French Revolution). A fifth and final Exposition Universelle took place in 1900, followed over the next half century by five International and Colonial Expositions of similar scale: the Exposition Coloniale (1907), the Exposition Internationale des Arts Décoratifs et Industriels Modernes (1925), the Exposition Coloniale Internationale (1931), the Exposition Internationale des Arts et Techniques dans la Vie Moderne (1937), and the Exposition Internationale de l'Urbanisme et de l'Habitation (1947).

The parade of expositions mounted between 1850 and 1950 necessitated increasingly large sites to accommodate the expanding breadth and quantity of their displays. Since few places within city limits could meet this requirement, organizers returned to prior sites that could accommodate not only vast exhibition halls but also a growing number of other pavilions and attractions.

As a measure of economy and practicality, many of the structures built for these fairs were conceived as semipermanent or permanent, becoming lasting urban presences and, in some cases, even beloved monuments. Two buildings from the 1855 Exposition, held in the

TOP: Evening reception at the second Exposition of French Industrial Products, held in the Cour Carrée of the Louvre, 1801.
BOTTOM: Publicity postcard depicting a bird's-eye view of the 1889 Exposition Universelle centered on the Eiffel Tower designed by Gustave Eiffel. Léonard Paupier was a manufacturer of weights and scales.

Jardin des Champs-Élysées near the Cours-la-Reine and the Place de la Concorde, offer a case in point: the Théâtre du Rond-Point still stands in the Rond-Point des Champs-Élysées, while the Palais de l'Industrie (Palace of Industry), a vast exhibition hall built on the Avenue des Champs-Élysées, served as the city's primary exhibition hall for nearly half a century before it was demolished.

The Champ-de-Mars was the site of both the 1867 and the 1878 Expositions. The latter, centered on a colossal Galerie des Machines, extended across the Seine by way of the Pont d'Iéna to the Trocadéro Gardens, where the Palais du Trocadéro housed a vast auditorium and exhibition space that were reused in later expositions. The 1889 Exposition occupied the same site as the 1878 Exposition, but also included a group of pavilions built along the Esplanade des Invalides. The main attraction in 1889 was the Eiffel Tower, now an indelible symbol of Paris.

The 1900 Exposition was by far the city's largest, encompassing the Champ-de-Mars, the Trocadéro, the Esplanade des Invalides, and the Place de la Concorde, as well as the banks of the Seine between them. The exposition saw the replacement of the old Palais de l'Industrie with the Grand Palais and the Petit Palais, as well as the newly built Pont Alexandre III linking the Place de la Concorde with the Esplanade des Invalides. The fair's immensity occasioned the introduction of the Rue de l'Avenir (the Street of the Future), a moving sidewalk over two miles long, carrying visitors between its multiple locations. The 1900 Exposition was accompanied by an Olympic Games, held in the Bois de Vincennes in the east of Paris.

Both the 1907 and the 1931 Colonial Expositions were also held in the Bois de Vincennes. Building elements from the 1907 Exposition remain in the park's Jardin d'Agronomie Tropicale. The magnificent Palais de la Porte Dorée, the principal exhibition and reception hall of the 1931 Exposition, still houses some of the finest and most complete French Art Deco interiors, most notably those designed by Ruhlmann and Eugène Printz.

TOP: View of the 1900 Exposition Universelle in Paris, centered on the Palais du Trocadéro exhibition hall designed by Gabriel Davioud with foreign pavilions in the foreground. BOTTOM: View of the Palais de Chaillot, built on the site of the Palais du Trocadéro for the 1937 Paris Exposition Internationale des Arts et Techniques dans la Vie Moderne by Louis-Hippolyte Boileau, Jacques Carlu, and Léon Azéma.

OVERLEAF: Bird's-eye view of the 1925 Paris Exposition. Watercolor by Jacques Henri Lambert.

Vue perspecti
Dessin aquarellé de J.-H. LAMBERT. — A droite et à gau

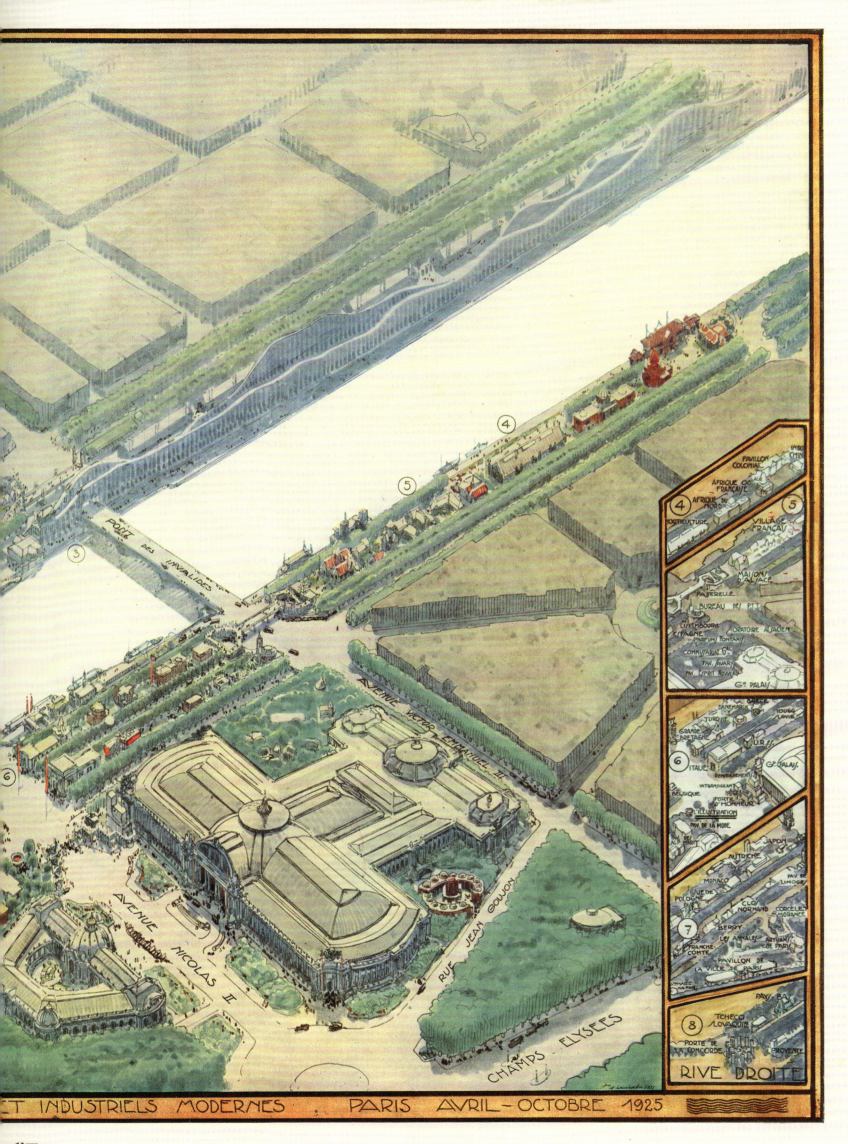

l'Exposition.
...mas et légendes désignant les pavillons et attractions.

The year 1937 marked the Exposition Internationale des Arts et Techniques dans la Vie Moderne (International Exposition of Art and Technology in Modern Life), which occupied a site running from the Champ-de-Mars across the Seine to the Trocadéro, extending along the riverbanks east and west of the Pont d'Iéna. For this exposition, the Palais du Trocadéro was torn down and replaced with the Palais de Chaillot, which today houses the Musée Nationale de la Marine, the Musée de l'Homme, and the Cité de l'Architecture et du Patrimoine.

The only postwar exposition in Paris took place in 1947: the Exposition Internationale de l'Urbanisme et de l'Habitation (the International Exhibition on Urbanism and Housing). Held in the Grand Palais and along the Cours-la-Reine, it occupied more or less the same site as the 1855 Exposition Universelle. Postwar austerity meant no new buildings were built for this final International Exposition.

The idea for the 1925 Exposition originated during the early twentieth-century reinvigoration of the French design industry. In 1912, the French government, with support from the Société des Artistes Décorateurs, agreed to sponsor an international exhibition of applied arts promoting French accomplishments in the field. Not surprisingly, with such governmental backing it would effectively function as a French trade fair, and the works exhibited—everything from architecture and interior design to jewelry and perfumes—would proclaim French supremacy in the production of luxury goods. Scheduled for 1915, the project was halted by the First World War.

Despite the emphasis on French goods, when planning was resumed after the war, more than twenty foreign countries were invited to participate in the 1925 Exposition. Prime sites were offered to France's major wartime allies: Belgium, Great Britain, Italy, and the United States. After much consideration, the American Secretary of Commerce, Herbert Hoover, and his committee of experts declined the invitation "on the ground that American manufacturers and craftsmen had almost nothing to exhibit conceived in the modern spirit and in harmony with the official specifications," curiously ignoring such important architect-designers as Frank Lloyd Wright.[7] Germany was pointedly excluded from the fair.

The 1925 Exposition was sui generis. Despite international participation, it was not an Exposition Universelle; although there was a colonial component, it was not a Colonial Exposition. Rather than presenting an expected mix of artistic and technological marvels, the exposition was self-defined by its title, specifying *arts décoratifs et industriels modernes*, or "modern decorative and industrial arts." Although the word *moderne* comes last in French, it is first and foremost in English. The organizers stipulated that everything exhibited had to be modern in conception. *Arts décoratifs* suggests ornament and embellishment, but the term is also synonymous with "applied arts" (as differentiated from the "fine arts" of painting and sculpture by the application of artistry and craftsmanship to utilitarian objects). The abbreviation *Art Deco* thus identifies *décoratif*—both literally and as a synonym for applied—as its distinguishing characteristic. The term *industriels* connotes a range of skills and techniques, from the handmade to the mass-produced, in all media. The Exposition proved that the decorative arts (and, more specifically, the luxury trades) were a significant economic force and a dependable income producer for designers and manufacturers alike.

The Exposition's displays encompassed every aspect of what in English might be described as the "built environment," but which the French poetically expressed as *les arts de vivre*: not only architecture,

– 32 –

Perfume display inside the Grand Palais, 1925 Exposition. Designed by Gilbert Raguenet and Camille Maillard.

gardens, interiors, and household furnishings, but also dining, fashion and beauty products, publishing, advertising, and transportation. Not included were the fine arts per se (such as easel painting or pedestal sculptures), science, technology, engineering, and medicine, except as they could be incorporated into the built environment. As at Salon exhibitions, displays ranged from individual objects to completely furnished environments.

Works were officially divided into five major groups: architecture, furnishings, dress, theatrical, street and garden arts, and education. These were further divided into thirty-seven classes, such as stonework, woodwork, metal, ceramics, glass, furniture, leather, and paper. Each class was overseen by a president, vice presidents, and reporters.

Rules governing what could be exhibited were specific:

> *Works admitted to the Exposition must show new inspiration and real originality. They must be executed and presented by the artists, artisans and manufacturers who have created models and by editors who represent the modern decorative and industrial arts. Reproductions, imitations and counterfeits of ancient styles will be strictly prohibited.*[8]

Although much of what the French exhibited was firmly rooted in tradition, the aesthetic unity of the exhibits indicates that Art Deco was a fully formed phenomenon by 1925. The United States government's official report on the Exposition put it more succinctly:

> *From all appearances the modern movement has been accepted to such a degree by the French people as to ensure its continued place in modern production in France and to establish it as the important note of design for the immediate future.*[9]

All in all, more than 15,000 exhibitors, both French and foreign, participated, and more than 7,000 prizes were awarded by the official juries. Everything displayed at the fair was for sale, and works were sold to both private buyers and museums.

The Exposition was presented under the official patronage of the Ministère du Commerce, de l'Industrie, des Postes et des Télégraphes and its minister, Charles Chaumet. Overseeing its organization was former Commerce Minister Fernand David. Reporting to him were Paul Léon, Dirécteur des Beaux-Arts (forerunner of the Ministry of Culture), and Alphonse Deville, a member of the Municipal Council of Paris. Other key players included François Carnot, president of the Union Centrale des Arts Décoratifs, who served as head of the admissions committee; architect Charles Plumet, as architect in chief; and landscape architect Jean-Claude Nicolas Forestier, who oversaw the gardens.

After considerable debate about where in Paris to mount the exhibition, a site at the city's center was

chosen. It extended north–south from the Grand Palais to the Invalides, incorporating both the Pont Alexandre III and the Pont des Invalides, and east–west along the Seine, from the Place de la Concorde to the Pont de l'Alma. On the Right Bank, it filled the parks of the Cours-la-Reine and the Cours Albert-1er, and on the Left Bank it lined the Quai d'Orsay. In addition to using the preexisting Grand Palais, more than 130 temporary

TOP: British pavilion. Designed by John Murray Easton and Howard Morely Robertson. MIDDLE: At left, Belgian pavilion. Designed by Victor Horta. At right, Japanese Pavilion (built on the site originally allocated to the United States). Designed by Yamada Shichigoro and Miyamoto Iwakichi. BOTTOM: Italian pavilion. Designed by Armando Brasini.

The four sites anchoring the corners of the Exposition's main axial crossing were assigned to France's principal allies in the First World War.

– 34 –

pavilions, arcades, gardens, barges, and entrance gates were newly built, and many of the buildings were divided into smaller boutiques, stands, and other displays. Most of the foreign pavilions were concentrated on the Right Bank near the Grand Palais, while French pavilions filled the Left Bank's Esplanade des Invalides and the quais on both sides of the river.

Some of the fair's French pavilions were organized by ensembliers, individual artist-craftsmen, manufacturers, and retailers, while others represented specific métiers, geographic regions, or professional associations. Foreign pavilions, understandably less ambitious than the French ones, mainly exhibited comparatively modest displays showcasing nationally characteristic work.

Many of the pavilions were built using molded reinforced concrete, an innovative material developed in the late nineteenth century and favored by progressive architects in the 1920s. Concrete could be left plain, embellished with surface decoration such as painting or sculpture, or clad in materials such as mosaic or marble. The nearly universal use of concrete united the otherwise aesthetically disparate pavilions.

Strict building regulations were imposed, stipulating precise heights and roofline restrictions. Existing trees and plantings could not be disturbed. These regulations were perhaps most visible along the axis of the Esplanade des Invalides, where low, horizontal pavilions with stepped, sloped, or domed roofs framed a view of the monumental Hôtel des Invalides designed by Jules Hardouin-Mansart in the late seventeenth century. This important landmark (conceived as a military hospital and home for veterans, it later came to house the tomb of Napoléon I) loomed above the Exposition as a reminder of the long French tradition of excellence in *les arts de vivre*.

The Porte d'Honneur, adjacent to the Grand Palais, was the Exposition's main entrance; from it, the central axis extended southward toward the Hôtel des Invalides. Just inside the gate was the Information Pavilion. The Grand Palais housed official reception spaces as well as extensive areas for displays.

TOP: The Rue des Boutiques, built along the Pont Alexandre III. Designed by Maurice Dufrène. MIDDLE: Porte d'Honneur (main entrance gate). Designed by Henri Favier, André Ventre, and Edgar Brandt. BOTTOM: Bird's-eye view of the Esplanade des Invalides.

These three images show aspects of the Exposition under construction.

The Cours-la-Reine—a park built for Queen Marie de' Medici in 1618, running along the right bank of the Seine between the Place de la Concorde and the Place du Canada—provided shady gardens that delighted visitors as well as a prestigious location for the foreign pavilions. Anchoring the main axis were sites assigned to Belgium, Great Britain, Italy, and the United States (when it declined to participate, its site was reassigned to Japan). Another entrance gate, designed by Pierre Patout, was prominently situated at the Place de la Concorde end of the Cours-la-Reine.

ABOVE: Porte d'Honneur (main entrance gate). Designed by Henri Favier, André Ventre, and Edgar Brandt. The frenetic pace of its installation caused certain elements of the gate to be fabricated in painted plaster rather than Brandt's signature wrought-iron, leading waggish artists in Montmartre to mount their own "Exposition des Arts Décors Hatifs" (Exposition of Hasty Arts) with displays made from cardboard and plywood, a caustic pun on the official fair's name.

OPPOSITE: The interiors of the Grand Palais—adjacent to the entrance gate— not only served as the official reception venue for the fair but also housed extensive displays of small-scale objects.

TOP LEFT: Decoration of the monumental staircase. Designed by Charles Letrosne. TOP RIGHT: Louis Vuitton display. MIDDLE LEFT: Main entrance hall. Designed by Charles Letrosne. MIDDLE RIGHT: Gala reception room. Designed by Louis Süe and Gustave Jaulmes. BOTTOM LEFT: Gallery of ceramics. Designed by Louis-Pierre Sézille et Henri Rapin. BOTTOM RIGHT: Hall of the metal and ceramics section. Designed by Louis-Pierre Sézille et Henri Rapin.

L'Esprit Nouveau pavilion. Designed by Le Corbusier and Pierre Jeanneret. One of the few unapologetically modernist buildings at the Exposition, this unusual design is centered on a tree growing through its roof. Regulations prohibited the removal of trees within the Exposition's footprint. The Grand Palais is visible behind the pavilion.

OPPOSITE: The Cours-la-Reine is a park that runs east-west along the right bank of the Seine, just inside the Exposition's main entrance gate; this area housed the majority of the international pavilions as well as numerous shady gardens.

TOP LEFT: Czech pavilion. Designed by Josef Gočár. TOP RIGHT: Garden. Designed by Joseph Marrast.
MIDDLE LEFT: Polish pavilion. Designed by Jósef Czajkowski. MIDDLE RIGHT: View of the Cours-la-Reine.
BOTTOM: Entrance gate at the edge of the Place de la Concorde. Designed by Pierre Patout.

Le Village Français (model of an archetypal French village) in the Cours Albert-1er. Designed by Charles Genuys and Adolphe Dervaux.

The Cours Albert-1er (dedicated in 1918 to the King of the Belgians) is the extension of the Cours-la-Reine, running from the Place du Canada to the Place de l'Alma. This area housed a variety of pavilions including those of the model *Village Français* and those of French colonies. Gate entrances were located at the Avenue Victor-Emmanuel III and along the Cours Albert-1er.

The north–south axis extended across the Pont Alexandre III and its Rue des Boutiques, an arcade of small shop-like displays. Barges were moored along the quais on both sides of the Seine, offering further displays and venues for restaurants and entertainments. Illuminated fountains lined the river.

Because existing railroad tracks ran along the left bank, the Quai d'Orsay housed transportation displays (as well as an amusement park). Subterranean tracks meant that trees could not be planted in this area, so garden displays were restricted to raised beds or potted plants Three gates served the Quai d'Orsay: at the Pont d l'Alma, at the Boulevard de la Tour-Maubourg, and at the Rue de Constantine.

OPPOSITE: Among the most interesting of the foreign pavilions in the Cours-la-Reine were those of Denmark, Sweden, and Austria, all designed by internationally renowned architects.
TOP: Danish pavilion. Architecture by Kay Fisker. Interior salon by Aage Rafn.
MIDDLE: Swedish pavilion. Architecture by Carl Bergsten. Salon de Dame interior by Uno Åhrén.
BOTTOM: Austrian pavilion. Architecture and salon interior by Josef Hoffmann.

– 40 –

The Esplanade des Invalides—centered on a lavish display presented by the Manufacture Nationale de Sèvres, its twin buildings designed by Patout—accommodated the majority of the French pavilions. Long galleries housing individual stands bordered the area, which had six entrance gates: one at each end of the Rue de l'Université and the Rue Saint-Dominique transverses, and two facing the Invalides in the Rue de Grenelle. Anchoring the northern half were the pavilions of the four major Paris department stores: Bon Marché, Printemps, Galeries Lafayette, and Grands Magasins du Louvre. Anchoring the southern half were four towers dedicated to France's wine-growing regions. At the south end of the esplanade was the exposition's most prominent pavilion, that of the Société des Artistes Décorateurs: the so-called *Ambassade Française* presented room settings for an idealized French Embassy, complete with state reception rooms and private family spaces, and the decoration of each room was carried out by a different member of the society.[10] Elsewhere were pavilions dedicated to French regions and cities (Nancy, Lyon-Saint-Étienne, Roubaix-Tourcoing, Mulhouse), métiers (diamond-cutting, glove-making, stained glass), and individual makers (Lalique, Süe et Mare, Fontaine).

OPPOSITE: The Seine was integrated into the Exposition by means of bridges, barges, and fountains set into the river itself.

TOP LEFT: Illuminated floating fountain in the Seine. Designed by Paul Poiret.
TOP RIGHT: Barge restaurant. Designed by Louis-Pierre Sézille.
BOTTOM: Amusement park on left bank of the Seine (Eiffel Tower in background). Designed by Charles Henri Besnard et al.

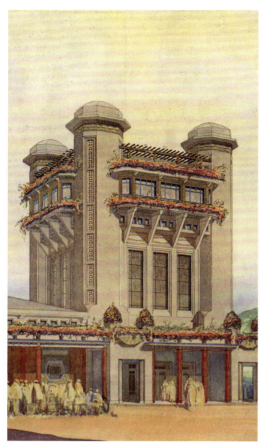

Porte Saint-Dominique-Fabert entrance gate. Designed by Joseph Marrast.

OPPOSITE: This group of pavilions and gardens—all of them French—were among those situated on the Esplanade des Invalides.

TOP LEFT: Tower. Designed by Charles Plumet. Watercolor by Louis Bailly.
TOP CENTER: Porte d'Orsay entrance gate. Designed by Louis-Hippolyte Boileau.
TOP RIGHT: Fountain. Designed by René Lalique. Watercolor by Henry de Renaucourt.
MIDDLE LEFT: Diamond Cutters pavilion. Designed by Pierre Bailly, Gustave Saacké, and Jacques Lambert.
MIDDLE RIGHT: Garden atop the train station terrace. Designed by Jacques Henri Lambert.
BOTTOM LEFT: Manufacture Nationale de Sèvres pavilion. Designed by Pierre Patout.
BOTTOM RIGHT: Galerie des Boutiques. Designed by Henri Sauvage.

The exposition enjoyed a second life in the United States when, in 1926, the American Association of Art Museums presented *A Selected Collection of Objects from the International Exposition of Modern Decorative and Industrial Art at Paris 1925*. This exhibition traveled to nine cities—Boston, New York, Cleveland, Chicago, Detroit, St. Louis, Minneapolis, Pittsburgh, and Philadelphia—attracting large crowds in each. Comprising nearly four hundred representative works, the exhibition curiously did not include any of its original complete room settings, a fundamental component of the displays in Paris.

Also on the Esplanade des Invalides were the pavilions for the interior design studios of the four major department stores in Paris.
LEFT: La Maîtrese pavilion for Galeries Lafayette. Architecture designed by Joseph Hiriart, Georges Tribout, and Georges Beau.
Hall interior designed by Maurice Dufrène.
RIGHT: Primavera pavilion for Printemps. Architecture designed by Henri Sauvage and Georges Wybo.
Hall interior designed by Alfred Levard.

In the following years, department stores across America recognized the commercial possibilities of importing and selling modern French designs. During the late 1920s, many retailers organized selling exhibitions (some of which included furnishings displayed at the 1925 Exposition, notably those by Ruhlmann) that served as much to inform and educate the public about modern design as to sell merchandise, on the assumption that while many visitors could not afford these modern objects, they were interested in contemporary design.

LEFT: Studium Louvre pavilion for Grands Magasins du Louvre. Architecture by Albert Laprade.
Boudoir interior designed by André Fréchet and Lahalle et Levard.
RIGHT: Pomone pavilion for Bon Marché. Architecture and hall interior designed by Louis-Hippolyte Boileau.

Musée d'Art Contemporain (Museum of Contemporary Art) pavilion. Architecture and interiors designed by Louis Süe and André Mare.

Manufacture Nationale de Sèvres pavilion. Architecture designed by Pierre Patout. Dining room designed by René Lalique with furniture by Charles Bernel.

Lalique pavilion. Architecture designed by Marc Ducluzaud with René Lalique. Dining room designed by René Lalique.

Salon inside the *Ambassade Française* pavilion of the Société des Artistes Décorateurs. Designed by Henri Rapin.

In response, American designers at first imitated what they saw coming from Europe with varying degrees of success. But as demand for modern products grew, Americans sought to find a design language that was uniquely theirs. Manufacturers in the United States understood that the French luxury model was ill suited to their country, which relied on middle-class consumers to buy their goods. Consequently, American Art Deco focused more on industrial designers—professionals engaged by manufacturers on a work-for-hire basis—and machine production than on ensembliers and artist-craftsmen.

Nonetheless, as the 1920s and 1930s progressed, a global taste for Art Deco—as first presented to the world at the 1925 Exposition—firmly established itself as a symbol of modernity. In some places, Mother Nature helped this process: the Great Japan Earthquake of 1923, the Great Miami Hurricane of 1926, and New Zealand's Hawke's Bay earthquake in 1931 all led to large-scale reconstruction projects that produced concentrations of Art Deco buildings. In cities such as Shanghai, Bombay, and Havana, global trade was the vector. Numerous World's Fairs—Barcelona (1929), Stockholm (1930), Chicago (1933–34), Paris (1937), San Francisco (1939), New York (1939–40), and Lisbon (1940)—all promoted Art Deco. By the Second World War, there was hardly a place where it could not be found.

E. J. Ruhlmann and Pierre Patout

The building that best epitomized the 1925 Exposition's (and French Art Deco's) tradition-based modernity was Ruhlmann's Hôtel du Collectionneur. Modeled on eighteenth-century pleasure pavilions, it was designed in collaboration with architect Pierre Patout to resemble a luxurious and modern private house. The project, which came at the midpoint of Ruhlmann's professional career, marks the pinnacle of his achievement as the preeminent ensemblier of his day. But who were Ruhlmann and Patout?

Jacques-Émile Ruhlmann (as he was christened) was born in Paris in 1879 and died there in 1933. There has long been debate over his correct appellation: he went through life known as Milo by family and friends, while professionally he referred to himself—on letterheads, business cards, and advertisements—as E. J. Ruhlmann or simply Ruhlmann.

He was brought up to inherit a household contracting firm founded by his mother's family in 1827; for nearly a century, it had offered standard services of the building trade: house painting, drywalling, wallpapering, mirror-making, and such. By the late nineteenth century, the business was being run by Ruhlmann's father, François, under whom the teenage Ruhlmann served an apprenticeship in the 1890s. In 1899, he met the fledgling architect Pierre Patout (1879–1965) during their compulsory military service.

Patout was the son of a surveyor from the French region of Burgundy (his father's career probably sparked an interest in his chosen calling). In 1896 he entered the Paris atelier of Jean-Louis Pascal, an architect trained in the classical tradition, and the following year enrolled at the École des Beaux-Arts in Paris. After their conscription, Patout introduced Ruhlmann to the profession of architecture by encouraging him to audit courses in Pascal's studio. Subsequently, an architectonic approach became fundamental to Ruhlmann's work. Thereafter, Ruhlmann and Patout were lifelong friends and frequent collaborators.

ABOVE: Pierre Patout in his office, 32 Rue Tronchet, Paris, ca. 1928.

OPPOSITE: E. J. Ruhlmann inside the Hôtel du Collectionneur, 1925.

LEFT: Exterior façade of the Établissements Ruhlmann et Laurent, Paris, ca. 1927. Designed by Pierre Patout.
RIGHT: E. J. Ruhlmann's sketches of *meubles précieux* (precious furniture).

In 1907, Ruhlmann married Marguerite Seabrook (1886–1957); following his father's death the same year, he took over the family business, ultimately reinventing its mission and turning it into one of the most celebrated decorating enterprises of its day. His earliest realized designs were wallpapers displayed at the 1911 Salon d'Automne where, in 1913, he presented his first complete interior, a dining room (he continued to participate in the annual Salon exhibitions until his death). Ruhlmann also began designing what he called *meubles précieux*, delicately attenuated furniture decorated with figurative motifs including dancing maidens, birds, or baskets of flowers. Hardly practical household furnishings, few pieces were made, but it was then that he began considering himself an ensemblier.

ABOVE: Advertisement for the Ruhlmann business, 1925. The lettering used in this advertisement would be adapted for the illuminated signs that crowned the Hôtel du Collectionneur at the 1925 Exposition.

OPPOSITE: *Tibattant* Desk, ca. 1923. Designed by E. J. Ruhlmann. Macassar ebony, ivory, leather, aluminum leaf, silver, and silk.

– 52 –

"L'HERBAGE" MAISON DE CAMPAGNE
à Lyons-la-Forêt (Eure)
Façades et plans de l'habitation

Trout fishermen's camp. Setting created by E. J. Ruhlmann for the 1932 Salon des Artistes Décorateurs.
For this exhibition, Ruhlmann created a complete interior for a rustic fishermen's camp. The project was regarded by critics as the antithesis of the Hôtel du Collectionneur.

Hall in Normandy, 1914. Designed by E. J. Ruhlmann.
Among his earliest designs, such rustic interiors were likely developed from studies for L'Herbage.

From the beginning of his career, Patout also regularly displayed his work at annual Salon exhibitions. Around 1910, together with fellow pupils from the Beaux-Arts, he established an architectural practice named Art et Construction. Among his earliest clients were Ruhlmann and his wife, for whom, between 1910 and 1913, he designed a country house, L'Herbage (The Pasture), in Lyons-la-Forêt, Normandy. Ruhlmann designed its interiors.

Chronic pulmonary issues plagued Ruhlmann throughout his life, and for much-needed rest he would retreat to L'Herbage, where he engaged in his favorite relaxing pastime of fly-fishing. His delicate health prevented him from serving in the First World War. Patout, however, like many creatives, served in the French army as a *camoufleur* (camouflage artist).

OPPOSITE: Photographs and floor plans of L'Herbage (The Pasture), 1913. Designed by Pierre Patout.
Ruhlmann's country house in Lyons-la-Fôret, Normandy, marked his first collaboration with his lifelong friend Patout.
It was to L'Herbage that Ruhlmann—who suffered from chronic pulmonary issues—retreated to fish trout throughout his life.

– 55 –

Showroom in the Établissements Ruhlmann et Laurent, 27 Rue de Lisbonne, Paris, ca. 1928.
Salon setting with furniture in macassar ebony, amaranth, and ivory.

In 1919, Ruhlmann joined forces with Pierre Laurent, who oversaw the lucrative household contracting side of their business. Ruhlmann himself added design studios, cabinetmaking and upholstery workshops, and a showroom. At its peak, their business employed upwards of fifty designers, craftsmen, and administrative staff. The Établissement Ruhlmann et Laurent produced much of their work in-house; what they could not do, such as the weaving of carpets and textiles or the manufacture of porcelain and glass, they contracted out to well-known makers: Cornille and Prelle for textiles, Defossé & Karth for wallpapers, and Sèvres for ceramics. In an operation of this size, Ruhlmann functioned as an editor, if not actually designing then overseeing and approving every aspect of a project or commission down to the smallest detail.

OPPOSITE: *État* Cabinet, designed 1922, manufactured 1925–26. Designed by E. J. Ruhlmann. Macassar ebony, amaranth, ivory, and silvered brass.
Ruhlmann gave this model its name because the French government purchased the first example.

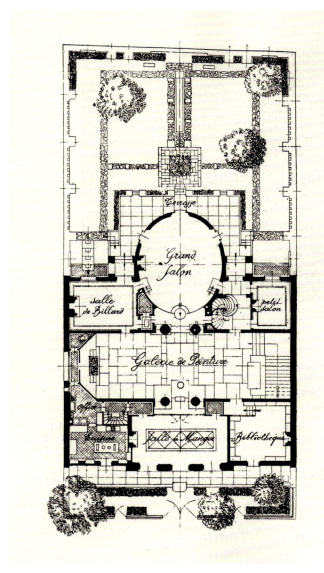

Entrance façade of the Gabriel Voisin residence, Boulogne ca. 1923. Designed by Pierre Patout. Interiors by E. J. Ruhlmann.

Ruhlmann quickly established a reputation as a designer of originality and skill. By 1920, articles praising his work appeared in the press. In 1922, one of his cabinets was acquired by the French state and in 1923 a desk was purchased by The Metropolitan Museum of Art. His work was displayed in numerous exhibitions in France and abroad. Private clients, mainly French, came to represent a veritable who's who of important figures in industry and business; foreign clients included the King of Siam and the Maharaja of Indore.

After the war, Patout opened his own firm, and over the next twenty years carried out a wide range of residential, commercial, and urban-planning projects. Among his prominent clients were airplane and automobile manufacturer Gabriel Voisin, for whom he designed a house in the Paris suburb of Boulogne in 1923, and textile manufacturer François Ducharne, for whom he designed a house in Paris in 1924; Ruhlmann executed interiors for both houses. In 1928, Patout remodeled the Ruhlmann et Laurent premises in the Rue de Lisbonne; two years later, he designed a house for politician André Tardieu, another client of Ruhlmann's.

OPPOSITE, TOP LEFT: Floor plan for the residence of textile manufacturer, François Ducharne, Paris, ca. 1926. Architecture by Pierre Patout. Interior design by Ruhlmann. TOP RIGHT: Entrance façade.
BOTTOM LEFT: Garden façade. BOTTOM RIGHT: View from grand salon through the gallery and into the dining room. Ruhlmann hung the grand salon's walls and upholstered the room's furniture with silks produced at the Ducharne factory in Lyons.

– 59 –

TOP LEFT: Sketch for *Élysée* Cabinet and *Cailloux* ("pebbles") marquetry. Drawing by E. J. Ruhlmann. TOP RIGHT: Sketch for *fuseau* (spindle) leg. Drawing by E. J. Ruhlmann. BOTTOM: *Élysée* Cabinet, 1920. Designed by E. J. Ruhlmann. Amboyna, ivory, and silvered bronze.

Fuseaux Cabinet, ca. 1925. Designed by E. J. Ruhlmann. Macassar ebony, ivory, silk, and silvered bronze.

Ruhlmann, while an excellent draftsman, was never a craftsman. Throughout his life, he kept notebooks filled with sketches (a sampling was published in the 1924 album *Croquis de Ruhlmann*). He also produced beautiful, finished drawings (many appeared in *Harmonies: Intérieurs de Ruhlmann*, also published in 1924) as he was building up his portfolio of clients. Such drawings reveal the careful attention he gave to all his projects. His design process invariably progressed from a tiny first sketch to larger working drawings and ended with full-scale details. This gradual process allowed every aspect of a project to be fully considered, from its overall effect to the most minute construction detail.

ABOVE: Directoire-style salon in the Duhem residence, Paris, ca. 1932. Designed by E. J. Ruhlmann.
Ruhlmann was comfortable incorporating a client's existing furniture, especially when it included antiques such as these. In this room, his contributions were restricted to the architectural details, which initially appear conventional but subvert norms by using over-scaled dentils running below the ceiling and wall panels wrapping around corners. The room was painted green-gray with details in gold leaf and curtains in green taffeta.

OPPOSITE: Drawings for the hall, salon, and dining room in the residence of Henri de Rothschild at the Chateau de la Muette in Paris.
These drawings illustrate Ruhlmann's ability, as an interior designer, to think like an architect.

Ruhlmann's work of the 1920s is considered his finest, embodying the combination of tradition and innovation that typify French Art Deco. But while many of the forms and decorative motifs he favored, not to mention the materials and construction techniques he employed, suggest those of the past, his furniture is unmistakably of the twentieth century and entirely original. He welcomed technical and material innovations (for example, preferring artificial sprays to natural lacquer) and enthusiastically addressed the incorporation of unsightly modern conveniences into elegant interiors (for example, reconfiguring radiators as freestanding bases for sculptures).

As Ruhlmann's reputation grew, so did the scope of his work. Increasingly, he played interior architect, reconfiguring spaces and floor plans to create luxurious sequences of rooms that flowed effortlessly from one to another. "One room, one space, cannot be considered in isolation," he stated. This important relationship, he argued, influenced function, circulation, furnishing plans, scale, tone, color, mood, and lighting. Neglecting it would result "in an overall impression of discord, a sense of crumbling and a lack of harmony in addition to a taste that is, at best, debatable."[11]

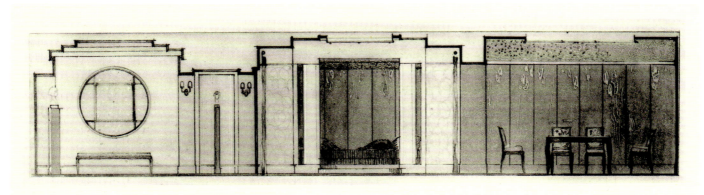

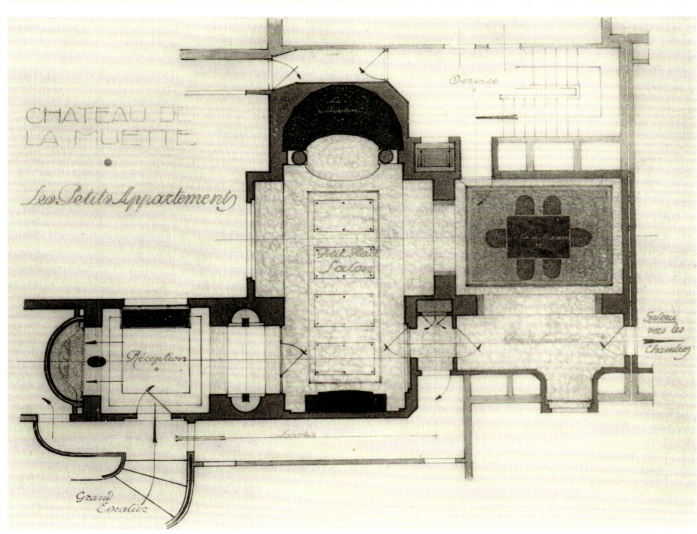

Petit salon in the residence of Lord Rothermere, Paris, ca. 1928. Designed by E. J. Ruhlmann. Reusing a chandelier from the Hôtel du Collectionneur, this room recalls the pavilion's boudoir.

Salon and dining room in the Lord Rothermere residence, ca. 1928. Designed by E. J. Ruhlmann. The dining room lamps were the same model Ruhlmann used in the 1925 pavilion, the furniture was lacquered red. The walls of the salon were paneled in palisander with silver-leaf details.

During the early 1920s, Ruhlmann developed his characteristic vocabulary of abstracted classicism. Wherever possible, rooms were symmetrical in both plan and elevation, although he favored unexpected shapes: ovals, circles, attenuated rectangles. Columns, paneling, and expanses of drapery brought stateliness to his interiors. "Observe how artfully our ancestors of the eighteenth century used verticals," he said, "achieving a sense of height and nobility . . . thus obtaining grandeur—because isn't seeing grand and being grand, for us, a dominant preoccupation?"[12] Nonetheless, his columns incorporated unorthodox capitals (or none at all), his wall panels turned with the room's corners (negating angles rather than defining them), spaces were delineated using pleated fabric hangings. While all these details evoked tradition, there was nothing overtly historicist in any of them.

Ruhlmann's made-to-measure furniture and interiors were expensive. He addressed his practice to a rarified clientele, and it was without irony that he stated:

> *Such ensembles do not address themselves to the middle classes; they are made for the elite. The rich client wants to possess only furniture that is impossible for the less rich to acquire. This furniture must therefore be costly, being difficult to execute and using precious materials that no knock-off can simulate.*[13]

Ruhlmann readily spoke of the huge amounts paid by French nobility for furniture by such eighteenth-century masters as André-Charles Boulle and Jean-Henri Riesener: "If you remark to Ruhlmann that he is not, in the strictest sense, in sync with his time, or rather with the trends of his time, he will readily remind you that the ancien régime created its masterpieces by throwing money at them, that Boulle received 95,000 livres for a cabinet for the Grand Dauphin, and Riesener 73,000 for Louis XV's desk."[14] Through such references, Ruhlmann not only compared himself to the greatest furnituremakers of the past, but also linked his patrons with royalty, a connection they were not likely to refute.

A gala reception room in the Chamber of Commerce and Industry of Paris, 1927. Designed by E. H. Ruhlmann.

Despite Patout's own taste for certain modernist trappings such as blank white walls and horizontal detailing, like Ruhlmann he maintained a healthy respect for tradition and classicism, favoring symmetrical compositions, regular rhythms, and monumentality. In 1926, he received the first of three commissions from the Compagnie Générale Transatlantique (CGT), builder of the French Line passenger ships: the first-class dining room, main foyer, and grand staircase on the *Île-de-France*, considered the first Art Deco ocean liner. (Ruhlmann would furnish the ship's first-class Salon Mixte.) The two commissions that followed were interiors and furniture for *L'Atlantique* and the *Normandie*, the benchmark of glamour in the era of ocean travel. Patout's work for the CGT influenced later projects such as his 1932 remodeling of the Galeries Lafayette department store on Boulevard Haussmann and a 1934 Paris apartment building that housed his own residence.

In 1928, Ruhlmann displayed a bedroom at the Salon des Artistes Décorateurs. For the first time, his room failed to impress critics, who had begun to tire of his particular brand of luxury and found the space ostentatious:

> *He piled up treasures, constructed an enormous shell worthy of a real Venus come back to earth, covered the walls with fabric having overwhelming motifs, hung from the ceiling a chandelier like a crystal fire, provided sculptured trophies. It was too much. This Olympian abandon displeased our spirit enamored by simplicity, at a moment when the innovators energetically preached great penitence and the benefit of asceticism in the decorative arts.*[15]

Given the climate of rapid political change and financial uncertainty, it is not surprising that Ruhlmann's most important commissions of the late 1920s and early 1930s were public ones: the gala reception rooms of the Chamber of Commerce and Industry of Paris in 1927, and the ceremonial office for Paul Reynaud (Minister of the Colonies) in the Palais de la Porte Dorée at the 1931 Exposition Coloniale (today, the only two extant Ruhlmann interiors). With their atmosphere of pomp and ceremony, such rooms projected a sense of security, stability, and confidence, representing the unassailable authority of the French state in a way that rivaled the interiors of Louis XIV's Palace of Versailles.

Salon de l'Afrique in the Palais de la Porte Dorée in Paris, 1931. Designed by E. J. Ruhlmann. Paintings by Louis Bouquet. Metal urns by Raymond Subes. This room served as both a ceremonial office for Paul Reynaud (Minister of the Colonies) and an exhibition room within the main reception building at the 1931 Exposition Coloniale. At the other end of a grand hall it was balanced by the Salon de l'Asie designed by Eugène Printz.

After a brief illness, Ruhlmann died in January 1933; he was interred in a tomb designed by his friend Patout. Under the supervision of his nephew and heir, Alfred Porteneuve, his business completed its outstanding projects and closed shortly thereafter. In 1934, a memorial exhibition organized by his widow was presented at the Louvre. Despite the criticism his work received in the years immediately before his death, Ruhlmann's contemporaries acknowledged his important role in the development of modern design. The art critic Marcel Zahar wrote:

> [Ruhlmann] shows us that one can love Versailles, sumptuous creations, beautiful materials, luxury, and rare and precious things and at the same time incorporate in one's present-day work the telephone, indirect lighting, scientific devices, central heating. But Ruhlmann never wished to depart from the principle of elegance. He sought not to interpret machine forms, but rather to establish the primacy of man and of taste over the machine—and that constitutes the most confounding problem of our time.[16]

For his contributions to French culture, Ruhlmann was made a Chevalier of the Légion d'Honneur in 1925 and an Officier in 1932.

Patout's work of the 1930s also focused on public commissions. Actively involved with the Société des Artistes Décorateurs, he designed its eponymous pavilion at the 1937 Paris Exposition. Another such project was the French pavilion at the 1939 New York World's Fair, designed in conjunction with Roger-Henri Expert, with whom he had previously collaborated on several ocean liner designs. Throughout the decade he was involved in urban-planning projects, redesigning the Longchamp corniche in the resort town of Saint Lunaire in 1931 and conceiving a new axial road linking Paris to the suburb of Saint-Germain-en-Laye in 1935. In 1940, he closed his Paris office. In 1946, he was appointed head architect for the reconstruction of the heavily bombed city of Tours where, in 1957, he built a new public library.

Given their prominence in 1925, it is not surprising that both Ruhlmann and Patout presented work in multiple locations at the Exposition. Ruhlmann furnished a study-library in the *Ambassade Française* pavilion (organized by the Société des Artiste Décorateurs), exhibited an *État* cabinet as part of the display of furniture masterpieces in the Grand Palais, and designed a piano for the Pleyel piano stand in the Rue des Boutiques that lined the Pont Alexandre III. Patout's most prominent contributions were the monumental entrance gate at the edge of the Place de la Concorde and the pavilion he designed, with architect André Ventre, for the Manufacture Nationale de Sèvres at the epicenter of the Esplanade des Invalides. He also designed a model electrical transformer building in the Cours Albert-1er and a small pavilion in the Cours-la-Reine for La Nacrolaque Jean Paisseau, a manufacturer of cellulose acetate used for products such as sequins and artificial pearls.

The project that brought the two friends together in 1925 was the Ruhlmann pavilion, built on a prime site on the main axis of the Esplanade des Invalides. Known officially as *L'Hôtel du Collectionneur* (the Collector's House), in period publications it was also called *Le Pavillon du Collectionneur* (the Collector's Pavilion) and *Le Pavillon d'un Riche Collectionneur* (the Pavilion of a Rich Collector). Designed to give the impression of a private mansion, it was described at the time as "a happy compromise between a real private house and an exhibition pavilion."[17] Official credit for the building and its contents was given to the Groupe Ruhlmann, an association of more than forty different designers, artists, and craftsmen working under the supervision of Ruhlmann, who himself played multiple roles in the creation of the pavilion.

Ruhlmann's tomb in the Passy Cemetery, Paris, 1933. Designed by Pierre Patout.
Both Ruhlmann and his wife, Marguerite, are interred in this tomb, which features a sculpture by Alfred Janniot (whose work Ruhlmann included in the Hôtel du Collectionneur) depicting a mourning woman holding an eternal flame. The recessed base of the tomb is embellished with a frieze of precisely engraved furniture details adapted from Ruhlmann's own drawings.

The Collector's House, 1925

The purported occupant of Ruhlmann's pavilion was an idealized collector—precisely the sort of person the exhibition was engineered to attract. That such a collector would be rich was a given, since the primary focus of the fair generally, and of Ruhlmann's pavilion specifically, was expensive luxury goods. But Ruhlmann himself also must be recognized as embodying this collector, since it was he who defined the pavilion's look and feel.

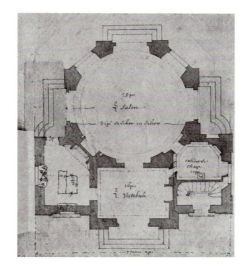  

Pavillon de Butard in the Bois des Hubies (Seine-et-Oise). Floor plan, elevation, and view of the salon (as it appeared ca. 1925). Designed by Ange-Jacques Gabriel in 1750 as a hunting lodge for King Louis XV.

While Patout designed the building's architectural framework, Ruhlmann was responsible for its overall conception. For years Ruhlmann had been working out ideas for an ideal house to serve as a model for the pavilion. A trial run of sorts came in 1924 when Ruhlmann and Patout collaborated on the François Ducharne residence, the design of which was remarkably like the Hôtel du Collectionneur, from its floor plan and exterior details to its interior furnishings. Drawings in Ruhlmann's sketchbooks depict small buildings set in formal gardens, some with French doors and stepped roofs. These sketches took inspiration from such eighteenth-century buildings as Ange-Jacques Gabriel's Pavillon du Butard and Pavillon de la Muette, royal hunting lodges built on the outskirts of Paris during the 1750s and 1760s, and François-Joseph Belanger's Château de Bagatelle, built by the Comte d'Artois in the Bois-de-Boulogne during the 1770s.

OPPOSITE: Floor plan of the Hôtel du Collectionneur, before 1925, showing Ruhlmann's ideas for furniture placements as the pavilion was being planned. Adapted from a drawing by Pierre Patout.

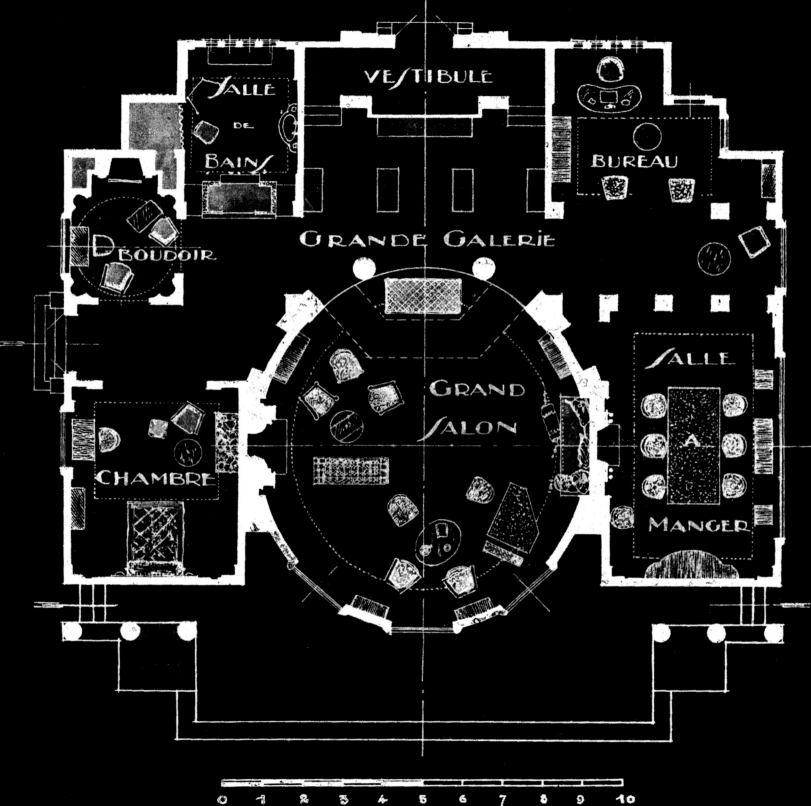

Garden elevation of the Hôtel du Collectionneur, before 1925. Designed by Pierre Patout.

Though Patout's building was faithful to Ruhlmann's vision of a modern-day pleasure pavilion, several details would be altered during the design process. A flat roof was replaced with a series of stacked platforms, and the two-story structure was reduced to a single floor to meet the exposition's rules for pavilions along the Esplanade des Invalides. Regulations imposed a height limit of 5.2 meters (approximately 17 feet) for the outermost façades, restricted the roofline angle to less than 45 degrees, and permitted roof heights of up to 10 meters (nearly 33 feet). Patout's revised roofline, reminiscent of a truncated pyramid, satisfied these requirements.[18]

The floor plan referenced eighteenth-century precedent, specifically the Pavillon du Butard. Dominated by a large, oval grand salon, it had an entrance vestibule and circulation corridor at one end; on one side were a dining room and study, and on the other side were a bedroom, boudoir, and bathroom. As the most important room, the grand salon was given the most impressive dimensions: its domed ceiling was 8 meters (more than 26 feet) high.[19] The other rooms, considered private spaces, were given modest dimensions—an eighteenth-century architectural planning device with which Ruhlmann and Patout were familiar. The lowest ceiling height of 2.5 meters (just over 8 feet) was in the bathroom.[20] There were no service rooms or kitchen, which in an eighteenth-century building would have been located on a lower floor, easily reached by a staircase.

The pavilion revealed several modernist conceits. Its simplified massing was underscored by Patout's use of plain reinforced concrete construction. The exterior composition reflected the distribution of the interior

Entrance front of the Hôtel du Collectionneur, 1925. Designed by Pierre Patout.
Clearly visible is the door marked ENTREE and the illuminated rooftop sign reading RUHLMANN. Another such sign was placed atop the garden façade.

rooms: the garden façade was dominated by the high, semicircular projecting bay of the grand salon that rose to the level of the highest platform, while the lower platforms indicate the diminishing scale of the rooms inside, with the lowest sheltering the most private rooms of the house. Window and door openings were treated similarly: monumental French windows opened from the grand salon, while smaller, screen-like openings brought light and privacy to the study and bathroom at the building's front.

Official regulations limited the inclusion of paintings and sculpture to those that were part of larger decorative schemes. In this spirit, Ruhlmann placed Alfred Janniot's large limestone sculpture *Spring (Homage to Jean Goujon)* beyond the grand salon terrace to suggest a garden. There was little other exterior decoration, save bas-relief panels by Joseph Bernard, which were set above both the entrance and the grand salon windows, and fresco panels by Henri Marret on the back walls of the two small columned porches of the terrace façade. Max Blondat's sculpture *L'Equilibre* (Balance) centered the garden in front of the pavilion's entrance, although this setting was presented as an independent exhibit by landscape architects Jules Vacherot and André Riousse.

OVERLEAF: Grand salon of the Hôtel du Collectionneur, looking toward the garden, 1925. Designed by E. J. Ruhmann.
In addition to his own furnishings, Ruhlmann selected objects by other designers. At left is a cabinet by Jean Dunand with a decorative motif
by Jean Lambert-Rucki; atop the cabinet is *Heracles the Archer*, a 1909 sculpture by Antoine Bourdelle. On the low table at center is *Ours Blanc* (Polar Bear),
a 1922 sculpture by François Pompon. Above the mantelpiece is *Les Perruches* (The Parakeets), a painting by Jean Dupas. The ceiling was painted
by Louis-Pierre Rigal, and the carpet was designed by Émile Gaudissard. The piano was made to Ruhlmann's design by Gaveau.

ABOVE: Grand salon of the Hôtel du Collectionneur, looking toward the grande galerie, 1925. Designed by E. J. Ruhmann. In addition to his own furnishings, Ruhlmann selected objects by other designers. The wrought-iron screen is by Edgar Brandt. At left is a cabinet by Léon Jallot, on which sits a bust by Alfred Janniot.
BELOW: *Les Perruches* (The Parakeets), a painting by Jean Dupas, was above the mantelpiece in the grand salon.

The richness of the pavilion's interior contrasted with the sobriety of its exterior. It represented Ruhlmann's skill as an ensemblier, his ability to provide every aspect of an interior from architectural details and furniture to textiles, lighting, paintings, sculpture, and objets d'art. While the undisputed centerpiece was the domed salon, each room was treated with the same degree of attention.

Ruhlmann's furnishings were sumptuous and, like the building's architecture, made a deliberate link with the past, both stylistically and intellectually. In the grand salon, a suite of seating furniture covered in tapestry and a monumental chandelier made from cascades of brilliant crystal prisms (hanging beneath a ceiling painted by Louis Pierre Rigal) recalled the grandeur and formality of the Empire and Louis Philippe periods. Throughout the pavilion, costly materials were used: precious wood veneers and lacquer for furniture, silk damasks and velvets for upholstery, furs for coverlets and throws.

OPPOSITE, TOP LEFT: *Ours Blanc* (Polar Bear), 1922. Designed and made by François Pompon. Bronze. TOP RIGHT: *Élégant* guéridon table, ca. 1913. Designed by E. J. Ruhlmann. Macassar ebony. MIDDLE LEFT: *Double Colonnettes* table, 1923. Designed by E. J. Ruhlmann. Mahogany, Macassar ebony, and ivory.
BOTTOM LEFT: Vase, 1925. Designed and made by Émile Lenoble. Glazed stoneware.
BOTTOM RIGHT: Cabinet, ca. 1925. Designed and made by Léon-Albert Jallot. Mahogany, palisander, and *Verde di Levanto* marble.

OVERLEAF: Study, 1925. Designed by E. J. Ruhlmann. In addition to his own furnishings, Ruhlmann selected objects by other designers. Léon Voguet designed the carpet. The 1910 sculpture *Jeune Fille à la Cruche* or *Porteuse d'eau* (Young Girl with a Jug or The Water Carrier) is by Joseph Bernard.

Dining room, 1925. Designed by E. J. Ruhlmann. In addition to his own furnishings, Ruhlmann selected objects by other designers. The bas-relief sculpture over the mantel is by Alfred Janniot. The tapestry is by Léon Voguet, and the carpet is by Émile Gaudissard. Silver objects are by Jean Puiforcat.

While Ruhlmann designed the majority of the pavilion's furnishings, in the spirit of his "collector" he also mixed in carefully selected works by respected contemporaries. Noteworthy were Edgar Brandt (ironwork), Émile Decœur (ceramics), François-Émile Décorchemont (glass), Jean Dunand (lacquer and metalwork), Léon-Albert Jallot (furniture), Francis Jourdain (outdoor furnishings), Pierre Legrain (bookbindings), Émile Lenoble (ceramics), Claudius Linossier (enamels), Jean Mayodon (ceramics), Jean Puiforcat (silver), and Henri Rapin (furniture). The inclusion of such pieces was determined by necessity as much as taste, to fully furnish the pavilion in time for the Exposition's opening.

OPPOSITE, TOP LEFT: *Bouillotte* Table Lamp, ca. 1925. Brass and painted brass.
TOP RIGHT: *Collectionneur* Desk, ca. 1925. Rosewood.
MIDDLE RIGHT: Pair of Lamps, ca. 1925. Silvered bronze and glass.
BOTTOM LEFT: *Palette* Dining Chair, ca. 1925. Macassar ebony.
BOTTOM RIGHT: *Collectionneur* Dining Table, ca 1925. Amboyna burl and brass.
All furnishings designed by E. J. Ruhlmann.

OVERLEAF: Bedroom, 1925. Designed by E. J. Ruhlmann. In addition to his own furnishings, Ruhlmann selected objects by other designers. The carpet is by Léon Voguet. At right, atop the cabinet, is *Perdrix* (Partridge), a sculpture by François Pompon.

Boudoir, 1925. Designed by E. J. Ruhlmann. In addition to his own furnishings, Ruhlmann selected objects by other designers. In the wall cabinets are glass objects by François-Émile Décorchemont. Different carpets were used in this room during the run of the Exposition; the carpet shown here is by Émile Gaudissard.

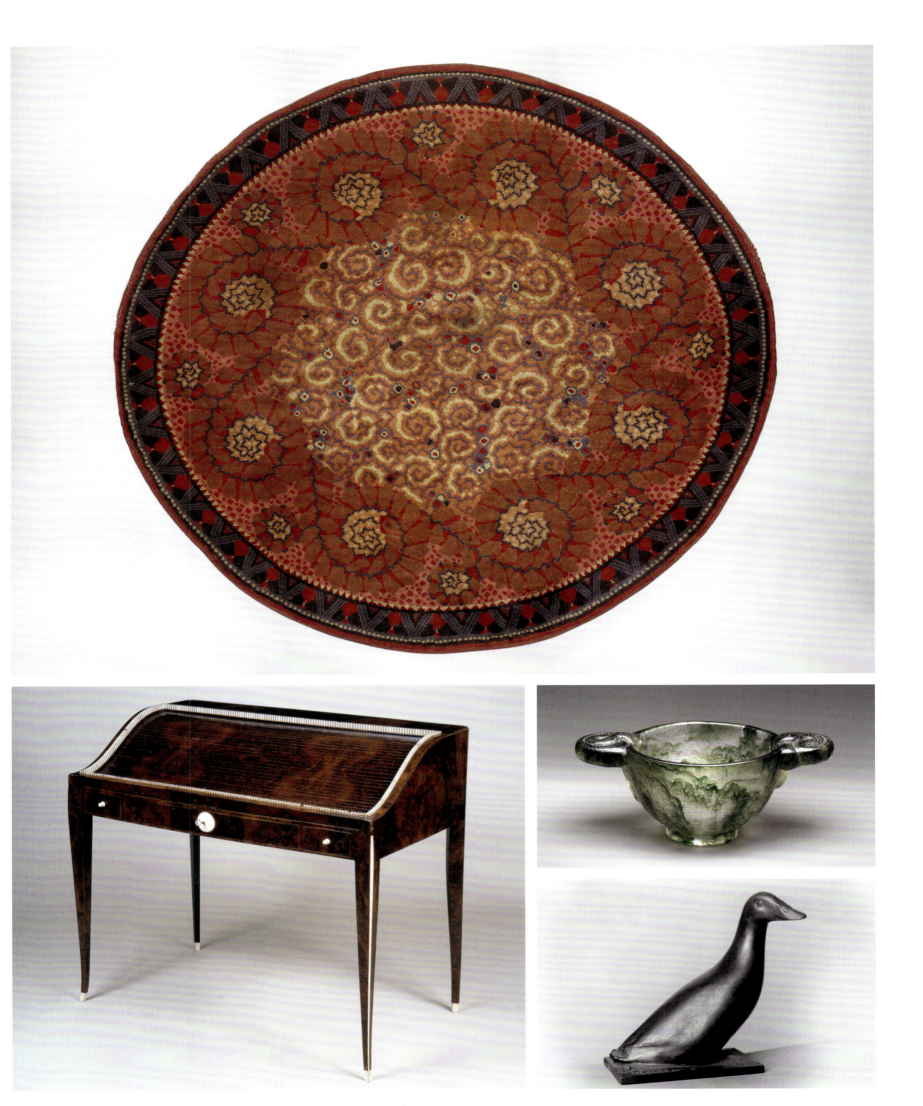

TOP: Carpet, ca. 1925. Designed by Émile Gaudissard for E. J. Ruhlmann. Wool and cotton.
MIDDLE RIGHT: Bowl, 1925. Designed and made by François-Émile Décorchemont. Glass.
BOTTOM LEFT: *Bureau de Dame* (Lady's Desk), 1923 (this example made in 1928). Designed by E. J. Ruhlmann. American walnut, Hungarian oak, and ivory.
BOTTOM RIGHT: *Canard sur l'Eau* (Duck on the Water), 1922. Designed and made by François Pompon. Bronze.

Exterior of the Hôtel du Collectionneur. Designed by Pierre Patout.
Clearly visible are the illuminated rooftop signs reading RUHLMANN and COLLECTIONNEUR. Another sign reading RUHLMANN was placed atop the entrance front. All three signs used the same lettering Ruhlmann chose for all his advertising.

Throughout the pavilion were paintings by Jean Dupas and Louis Pierre Rigal and sculptures by Joseph Bernard, Antoine Bourdelle, Alfred Janniot, and François Pompon. While such art may not have represented the most avant-garde taste of the period, its decorative effect harmonized with Ruhlmann's vision. He brought the eye of a seasoned decorator to their selection.

The Établissements Ruhlmann et Laurent (the household contracting side of Ruhlmann's business, run by Pierre Laurent) attended to painting, gilding, and mirroring needs. Two Ruhlmann clients also contributed services: M. Zell, a plumbing supplier who commissioned a Paris showroom from Ruhlmann, provided heating, plumbing, and bathroom fixtures; M. Berger, a timber merchant for whom Ruhlmann decorated an apartment, provided the building's wood framing and interior paneling.

Spring (Homage to Jean Goujon), 1925. Designed and made by Alfred Janniot. Painted limestone.
Ruhlmann selected this sculpture by his friend Janniot and placed it prominently outside the pavilion's garden façade. The sculpture was an homage to the famed French Renaissance sculptor Jean Goujon. It represents Diana the Huntress flanked by nymphs with a buck at her feet.

Although Ruhlmann had earned a lofty and widespread reputation long before the Exposition, he used his pavilion as an opportunity to burnish it in dazzling physical terms. Gilding the lily, he crowned the building with signs in small lights: RUHLMANN atop both the main entrance and garden façade, and COLLECTIONNEUR along its Esplanade roofline.

Like all the pavilions, the Hôtel du Collectionneur was torn down after the fair closed. It existed for only six months, although furnishings from it survive in museums including the Musée des Arts Décoratifs in Paris, the Calouste Gulbenkian Museum in Lisbon, the Casa de Serralves in Porto, and The Metropolitan Museum of Art in New York—as well as in private collections around the world. Its most lasting record exists in *L'Hôtel du Collectionneur*, the commemorative book published in 1926 by Éditions Albert Lévy. But even only as a memory, Ruhlmann's pavilion represents perhaps the most complete and elegant expression of Art Deco taste, one of the significant aesthetic achievements of its age.

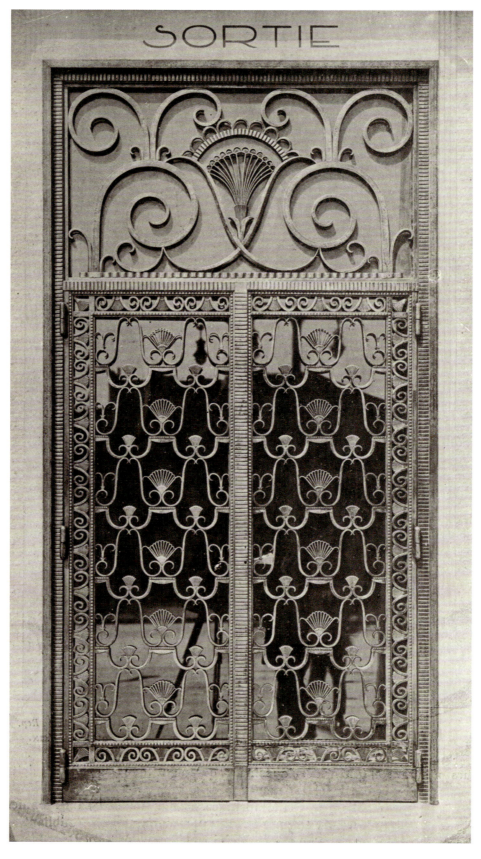

Exit door of the Hôtel du Collectionneur, 1925. Designed and made by Edgar Brandt.
The main entrance door was marked ENTREE while the exit door (on the side facing the Esplanade)
was marked SORTIE, indicating strictly controlled circulation.

EXPOSITION · DES · ARTS · DECORATIFS · MIL · NEUF · CENT · VINGT · CINQ

L'HOTEL DU COLLECTIONNEUR

GROUPE RUHLMANN

préface de Léon Deshairs, conservateur de la bibliothèque des arts décoratifs

EDITIONS ALBERT LEVY

2 RUE DE L'ECHELLE PARIS

L'HÔTEL
DU
COLLECTIONNEUR

*Les modèles publiés dans le présent ouvrage sont et demeurent
la propriété de leurs auteurs, toutes reproductions, même partielles,
sont interdites et seront poursuivies par les auteurs.*

EXPOSITION DES ARTS DÉCORATIFS DE 1925

L'HÔTEL DU COLLECTIONNEUR

GROUPE RUHLMANN

Décorateur : RUHLMANN, maître de l'œuvre. — *Architecte :* PATOUT
Sculpteurs : J. BERNARD, BOURDELLE, DEJEAN, DESPIAU, FOUCAULT, HAIRON, JANNIOT, LE BOURGEOIS, POISSON, POMPON, TEMPORAL. — *Peintres :* BONFILS, DEGALLAIX, DUPAS, GAUDISSARD, JAULMES, MARRET, REBOUSSIN, RIGAL, RUDNICKI, STEPHANY, L. VOGUET.
Décorateurs : BOILEAU, CARRIÈRE, L. JALLOT, FRANCIS JOURDAIN, RAPIN.
Orfèvre : PUIFORCAT. — *Ferronnier :* EDGAR BRANDT. — *Céramistes :* DECŒUR, LENOBLE, MAYODON. — *Dinandiers :* J. DUNAND, CL. LINOSSIER. — *Verrier :* DÉCORCHEMONT.
Relieurs : KIEFFER, LEGRAIN. — *Tablettiers :* BASTARD, Mme O'KIN

PRÉFACE DE LÉON DESHAIRS
Conservateur de la Bibliothèque des Arts Décoratifs

ÉDITIONS ALBERT LÉVY — 2, RUE DE L'ÉCHELLE, PARIS

Copyright by EDITIONS ALBERT LÉVY, 1926.

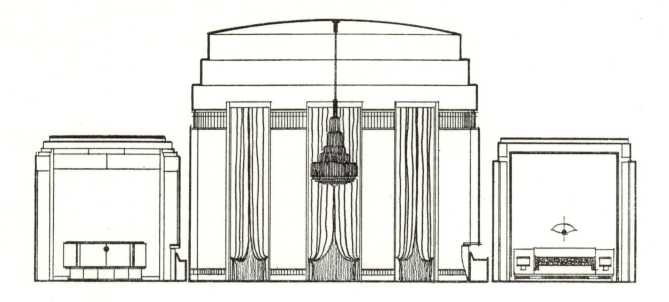

Quel collectionneur? Un collectionneur imaginaire et cependant très vivant. Il ne se complaisait pas, comme tant d'autres, dans le seul décor du passé. Il aimait les choses de son temps et faisait parmi elles un choix judicieux. De plus, il voulait que, dans sa maison, tout, murs, tapis, tissus, meubles, peintures, sculptures, bibelots de vitrines, fût intimement accordé. Il voulait qu'il y eût harmonie entre l'architecture de sa demeure et les objets d'art qu'il y réunissait pour sa joie. A tous égards donc, ce collectionneur avait droit au meilleur accueil à l'Exposition internationale des arts décoratifs et industriels modernes.

Ce collectionneur, c'est Ruhlmann qui l'inventa. Et, en créant ce personnage, il obtint un double succès : il put, à la fois, rester l'artiste que l'on connaît, et se conformer très exactement au programme initial de l'Exposition. Sans rien abdiquer de son goût pour un luxe raffiné, pour une simplicité précieuse, sans renoncer à sa fantaisie originale, Ruhlmann appliqua, autant ou mieux que personne, les principes d'une manifestation où les œuvres relevant des diverses techniques devaient, déclarait-on à l'origine, être présentées, autant que possible, « en fonction de la vie, c'est-à-dire comme elles le sont dans la réalité, suivant leur destination, leur emploi, en un ensemble créant le décor de notre existence quotidienne ».

On eût été surpris si Ruhlmann avait proposé de construire une maison ouvrière et d'y exposer des meubles à bon marché. Non qu'il méconnaisse l'utilité sociale de telles applications de l'art; non qu'il ne sache que l'objet le plus simple, la matière la plus commune peuvent être ennoblis par un reflet de l'intelligence et du talent. Mais d'autres soins le sollicitent. Il aime les bois précieux incrustés d'ivoire, les subtils rapports de couleurs, l'ébénisterie savante au service d'un dessin pur, les ouvrages où la construction n'est pas brutalement apparente, où l'effort demeure caché. Les meubles nés de ses recherches, joints à quelques-uns de ceux qu'il admire dans la production de ses émules, les œuvres d'art de toute sorte dont il se plait ou se plairait à s'entourer, il imagina de les grouper dans l'hôtel d'un amateur hypothétique qui lui eût ressemblé comme un frère.

Pour bâtir la maison de ce Mécène d'espèce rare, Ruhlmann n'avait pas à chercher bien loin un architecte; il s'adressa à son ami Pierre Patout. Pour la meubler et pour l'orner, il réunit les œuvres ou coordonna les efforts d'une quarantaine d'artistes et d'autant d'industriels. Ainsi fut réalisé l'attrayant ensemble que les visiteurs de l'Exposition de 1925 n'ont pas oublié. Ruhlmann en avait été à la fois l'initiateur, le maître-d'œuvre et le plus actif ouvrier. Si, dans ce détail encore, il n'eût cherché et trouvé une solution élégante, il eût pu s'abstenir de tracer les lettres de son nom, au couronnement de l'édifice, en un pointillé lumineux : quel homme un peu accoutumé à l'art français moderne n'y eût reconnu partout sa direction ou sa main ?

Le Mécène idéal n'avait que deux imperfections : il ne pouvait ouvrir au maître de l'œuvre un crédit aussi large que celui-ci l'eût souhaité et il n'était pas entièrement libre, puisqu'il devait compter, en plan et en élévation, avec des limites imposées. Mais les contraintes matérielles stimulent l'ingéniosité. Si Pierre Patout n'a pas pu édifier une maison aussi complète et habitable qu'il l'aurait voulu, s'il a remplacé le béton ou la pierre par le plâtre et le staff, matériaux des constructions éphémères, enfin s'il n'a pas vu ses blanches façades dans la verdure d'un parc, au milieu des pelouses et des parterres qui eussent été leur cadre naturel, reconnaissons qu'il a réalisé un heureux compromis entre l'hôtel vrai et le pavillon d'exposition. Dans un carré du 18 mètres de côté, ou plutôt dans un octogone, car les angles du carré devaient être abattus pour faciliter la circulation de la foule, il a su distribuer commodément un vestibule, une galerie où le collectionneur avait dressé quelques vitrines, un grand salon ovale à coupole, éclairé par trois hautes portes-fenêtres s'ouvrant sur le parc supposé. Puis, à droite de l'axe principal, une salle de bains, un boudoir, une chambre; à gauche, un bureau et une salle à manger : toutes pièces d'un caractère bien approprié à leur destination et de proportions agréables.

Pour l'harmonie de l'esplanade des Invalides, un *gabarit* était imposé à l'architecte : les façades de son pavillon ne devaient pas s'élever à plus de 5 mètres 20; la couverture — toit, dôme ou terrasse — ne pouvait dépasser une ligne idéale formant, avec l'horizontale, un angle de 45 degrés. Pierre Patout aurait pu couronner l'Hôtel du Collectionneur par une calotte analogue à celle du pavillon Süe et Mare ou par un cône tel que celui dont Sauvage, afin d'utiliser tout le volume, coiffa le pavillon du « Printemps. » Il opta pour un système de terrasses superposées, une sorte de pyramide tronquée, aux lignes fermes, faite de trois hauts gradins et terminée par une plate-forme. La coupole du salon ovale montait sous la plus haute terrasse, tandis que, sous la plus basse, s'abritaient les pièces destinées à la vie intime. D'autre part, la façade opposée à l'entrée était légèrement en retrait sur un des côtés du carré concédé au « groupe Ruhlmann ». Quitte à perdre, en plan, un peu d'espace, l'architecte avait adopté ce parti afin de pouvoir, sans dépasser le *gabarit,* élever plus haut le mur et les trois portes-fenêtres du salon ovale.

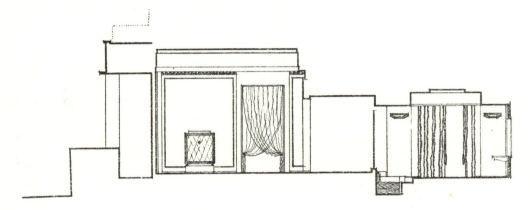

Ainsi l'Hôtel du Collectionneur n'était pas une création de la libre fantaisie. Son plan exprimait un programme; ses élévations correspondaient au plan. L'aspect extérieur de l'édifice avait été, dans une large mesure, déterminé à la fois par la distribution et la forme des pièces et par les limites idéales que traçait le *gabarit.* Le goût de l'architecte avait fait le reste. Il se manifestait d'abord par la recherche des contrastes qui bannissent la monotonie, font grand, même dans un petit espace, donnent, comme on dit, « de l'échelle » : Les pleins prédominaient nettement sur les vides; des fenêtres étroites s'ouvraient non loin d'une large baie; un mur courbe, animé par trois hautes ouvertures et par une frise en bas-relief, se dressait entre deux portiques bas. Ce goût se reconnaissait encore à la sobriété ornementale. Peu d'éléments décoratifs, mais bien choisis et bien placés : les bas-reliefs de Joseph Bernard, les portes en fer forgé et les balcons d'Edgar Brandt. Les grands nus n'étaient même pas coupés par l'ombre mouvante d'une corniche; celle-ci était remplacée par un bandeau plat. Enfin ce pavillon d'un dessin fin et net, était à la fois très neuf et traditionnel. Avec son salon ovale, son boudoir, la discrétion de son décor, ne rappelait-il pas librement quelque « folie » du XVIIIe siècle français?

Bien close, cette maison dédiée à l'art piquait la curiosité. Ses dehors étaient assez simples pour ne pas constituer à eux seuls tout le spectacle, ornés avec assez d'amour pour qu'on désirât voir, au dedans, la fête de beauté pressentie. On entrait et, à peine franchi le vestibule tendu de toile grise, on éprouvait une impression de luxe exquis. Là, Ruhlmann avait rassemblé les meubles de la forme et du travail le plus achevés, les siens, ceux de Jallot, de Rapin, un paravent en laque de Dunand. Là il avait joué en maître des rappels et des contrastes. A côté du haut salon ovale, toutes les autres pièces paraissaient plus intimes. Chacune avait sa couleur, son atmosphère. Sous la coupole du grand salon, peinte par Rigal d'ocres et de violets, les murs étaient tendus d'un beau damas gris-argenté, composé par Stephany, et le tapis de Gaudissard mêlait, sur un fond gris, les bleus et les roses. Un douce clarté blonde régnait dans la chambre où le lit et la commode étaient en bois d'amboine, la tenture murale de damas crême, à reflets nacrés. Le gai boudoir relevait son harmonie blanc, or et vert, par de petits meubles noirs. La salle à manger, aux murs revêtus de *lap* brun-rouge, avait été voulue assez sombre, reposante aux yeux...

Tel était le cadre où Ruhlmann avait présenté avec art, à la faveur d'éclairages variés et parfois de mystérieux contre-jour, une collection vivante et de qualité rare que je n'entreprendrai pas de décrire. L'Hôtel du Collectionneur n'est plus. Il n'a vécu que six mois. Puisse-t-il avoir préparé des réalisations plus durables. Moderne, mais d'un modernisme sous outrance, sans austérité agressive, il a, dans son existence trop brève, résumé quelques-uns des raffinements d'aujourd'hui.

LÉON DESHAIRS.

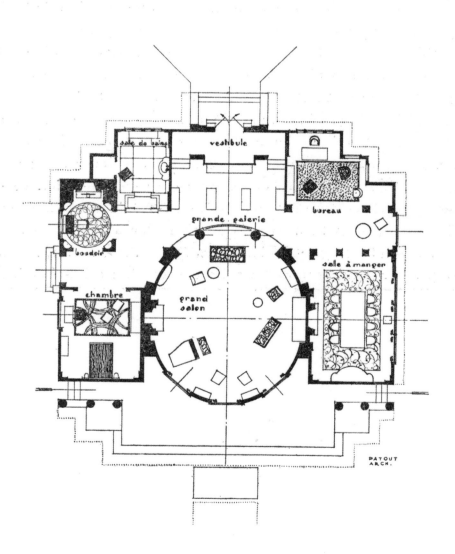

L'HOTEL DU COLLECTIONNEUR. — I.

L'HOTEL DU COLLECTIONNEUR. — II.

L'HÔTEL DU COLLECTIONNEUR. — III.

L'HOTEL DU COLLECTIONNEUR. — IV.

L'HOTEL DU COLLECTIONNEUR. — V.

L'HOTEL DU COLLECTIONNEUR. — VI.

L'HÔTEL DU COLLECTIONNEUR. — VII.

L'HOTEL DU COLLECTIONNEUR. — VIII.

L'HÔTEL DU COLLECTIONNEUR. — IX.

L'HOTEL DU COLLECTIONNEUR. — X.

L'HOTEL DU COLLECTIONNEUR. — XI.

L'HOTEL DU COLLECTIONNEUR. — XII.

L'HOTEL DU COLLECTIONNEUR. — XIII.

L'HOTEL DU COLLECTIONNEUR. — XIV.

L'HOTEL DU COLLECTIONNEUR. — XV.

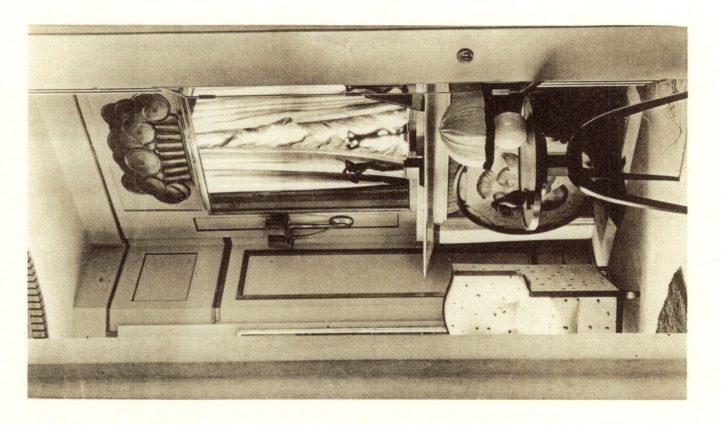
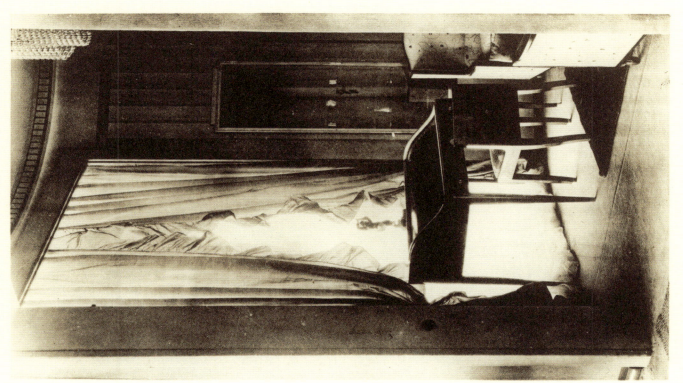

L'HÔTEL DU COLLECTIONNEUR. — XVI.

L'HOTEL DU COLLECTIONNEUR. — XVII.

TABLE DES PLANCHES

Frontispice.   *Grand salon.*

Planche   I.   *Projet primitif.* — Patout, architecte.

Planche   II.   *Façade principale.* — Patout, architecte.

Planche   III.   *Façade sur le jardin* — Patout, architecte.

Planche   IV.   *Grand salon.*

Planche   V.   *Grand salon.*

Planche   VI.   *Grand salon.*

Planche   VII.   *Détail du plafond du grand salon.* — Rigal, peintre.

Planche   VIII.   *Salle à manger.*

Planche   IX.   *Salle à manger, détails.*

Planche   X.   *Bureau.*

Planche   XI.   *Bureau.*

Planche   XII.   *Chambre à coucher.*

Planche   XIII.   *Chambre à coucher, détail.*

Planche   XIV.   *Chambre à coucher, coiffeuse.*

Planche   XV.   *Boudoir.*

Planche   XVI.   *Boudoir, détails.*

Planche   XVII.   *Salle de bains.*

TYPOGRAPHIE ET TRICHROMIE G. KADAR
42, RUE FALGUIÈRE, A PARIS
PHOTOTYPIE JACOMET, 68, RUE ERLANGER
A PARIS

L'Hôtel du Collectionneur translation

✣

Who is this collector? He is a collector at once imaginary and yet very much alive. Unlike so many others, he doesn't merely take pleasure in the styles of the past. He likes things of his own time, and from them he chooses judiciously. Furthermore, he wants everything in his house—walls, carpets, furniture, paintings, sculptures, bibelots—to complement one another meticulously. He desires harmony between the architecture of his home and the objets d'art that he has gathered within it for his own delight. In every respect, then, does such a collector deserve the warmest welcome at the International Exhibition of Modern Decorative and Industrial Arts.

It was Ruhlmann who conjured up this collector. And in creating this character, he achieved a double success: both managing to remain the artist we know so well and complying precisely with the exhibition's basic program. Without relinquishing any of his taste for refined luxury or precious simplicity, without renouncing the originality of his imagination, Ruhlmann observed, better than anyone else, the exhibition's original guiding principle, wherein works would showcase a variety of techniques but would also be presented as, and to the greatest extent possible, "functional for real life, which is to say just as they would exist in reality, suited to their placement and usage in an ensemble that re-creates the décor of our everyday lives."

One would have been surprised had Ruhlmann proposed building a worker's house, displaying inexpensive furniture inside. It's not that he disregards the social value in using his skills to such ends; nor does he lack an understanding of how the simplest object, or the most ordinary material, can be ennobled by

Exterior view of the Hôtel du Collectionneur, 1925. Designed by Pierre Patout.

All images on pages 137–40 are reproductions of period autochromes—an early glass-plate, color photographic process.

means of careful consideration and know-how. But other things beckon him: He loves precious woods inlaid with ivory, subtle plays of color, expert cabinetmaking emphasizing a clean design, works whose construction techniques aren't blatantly obvious—where effort is hidden. Furniture of his own conception, a selection of admirable pieces made by his colleagues, and a wide range of artworks that delight him and that he is happy to have around him—he imagines gathering all these things in the house of this hypothetical art lover, who resembles him closely enough to be his brother.

To build the house for this rare sort of patron, Ruhlmann didn't have to look far to find his architect; he turned to his friend Pierre Patout. To furnish and decorate it, he brought together and coordinated the work of about forty artists and as many tradesmen. Thus, he was able to realize the beautiful ensemble that visitors to the 1925 Exposition haven't forgotten. Ruhlmann himself was at once the initiator, the project manager, and the most active participant, to such an extent that even if he had not looked for and found an elegant solution for this one final detail, he could have refrained from spelling out his name in illuminated letters that ran along the building's cornice. For what person even minimally acquainted with modern French art wouldn't have recognized Ruhlmann's eye and hand everywhere?

This imaginary Maecenas has only two flaws: He wasn't able to provide the master-creator with pockets as deep as he might have wished, nor did he have carte blanche (for the design), being obliged to consider the restrictions imposed on both plan and elevation. But material constraints stimulate ingenuity. Even though Pierre Patout wasn't able to build a house quite as complete and livable as he might have liked, even though he had to replace concrete and stone with plaster and staff, the materials of ephemeral structures, and—finally—even though he wasn't able to see his white façades set within the greenery of

LEFT: Grand salon mantelpiece in the Hôtel du Collectionneur with Jean Dupas painting, 1925. RIGHT: Boudoir.

a garden, amid the lawns and parterres that should have been their natural framework, one must admit that he has achieved a happy compromise between a real house and an exhibition pavilion. In a square plot 18 meters across, more or less octagonal in shape because the corners of the site had to be cut off in order to facilitate the circulation of the crowds, he was able to commodiously arrange a vestibule, a gallery where the collector has installed some display cases, and an oval, domed grand salon, lit by three high French doors that open onto the notional garden. To the right of the main axis are a bathroom, a boudoir, and a bedroom; to the left, a study and a dining room: Each room is designed in a manner well_suited to its purpose, with pleasing proportions.

To maintain harmony along the Esplanade des Invalides, constraints were imposed on the architect: The façades of his pavilion could not be higher than 5.2 meters; the roofline—whether sloped, domed, or stepped—could not exceed a pitch of more than 45 degrees from horizontal. Pierre Patout might have crowned the Hôtel du Collectionneur with a small dome, like that on the Süe et Mare pavilion, or with a cone, such as the one Sauvage used, to top the Printemps pavilion to make use of the entire volume. Instead, he opted for a scheme of stacked terraces, (creating) a sort of truncated pyramid with strong lines, consisting of three principal tiers terminating with a platform. The cupola of the oval salon rose up into the highest terrace, whereas the rooms allocated to private life were sheltered beneath the lowest one. Furthermore, the (garden) façade, on the side opposite the entrance, recedes slightly from the edge of the site given to the "Ruhlmann Group." Willing to sacrifice a bit of space in the floor plan, the architect has adopted this scheme so as to raise to a great height the walls and three French doors of the oval salon, without exceeding the limitations of the constraints.

Thus, the Hôtel du Collectionneur was not a creation of fantasy. Its plan expressed its program; its elevations corresponded to its plan. The building's external appearance was, in large part, determined both by the arrangement and shape of the rooms, as well as by the standardized restrictions that determined its (overall) outline. The taste of the architect did everything else. His taste is revealed in the well-considered contrasts that relieve monotony, widely used (even in small spaces) and imposing, as one might say, "a sense of scale." Solids clearly predominate over voids; narrow windows open not far from a wide bay; a curved wall, enlivened by three tall openings and surmounted with a bas-relief frieze, stands between two low porticoes. His taste is also evident in the building's ornamental sobriety.

Garden adjacent to the Hôtel du Collectionneur, 1925. Designed by Vacherot and Riousee. Looking in from (top) and out toward (bottom) the Esplanade des Invalides.

– 139 –

Although there are only a small number of decorative elements, these are well chosen and well placed: bas-reliefs by Joseph Bernard, wrought-iron door grilles and balconies by Edgar Brandt. The large, blank wall surfaces themselves are not even broken up by the moving shadow of a cornice, which has been replaced by flat banding. In short, this pavilion, with its refined and pure design, is at once entirely new and quite traditional. With its oval salon, its boudoir, and the reserved nature of its décor, does it not recall a few of the "follies" of eighteenth-century France?

Once completed, this house devoted to art piqued curiosity. Its exterior was simple enough not to constitute the entire spectacle in and of itself but rather was adorned with sufficient loving attention that one wished to see the hinted-at celebration of beauty inside. You entered and, hardly having passed into the vestibule hung with gray cloth, you felt an impression of exquisite luxury. There, Ruhlmann brought together a group of furniture of the most elegant design and accomplished workmanship, both his own pieces and those of Jallot, of Rapin, a lacquered screen by Dunand. There, he played the role of master in assemblages and contrasts. Next to the lofty oval salon, all the other rooms appeared quite intimate. Each had its own color scheme, its own atmosphere. Beneath the grand salon's cupola, painted by Rigal in tones of ochre and violet, the walls were hung with a handsome silvery-gray damask designed by Stephany, and the carpet by Gaudissard blended blues and pinks on a gray ground. A soft, pale mood prevailed in the bedroom, where the bed and the commode were made from amboyna wood, and the wall hangings were of cream-colored damask with a pearly glow. The cheerful boudoir offset its harmonious white, gold, and green color scheme with small, black furniture. The dining room, with its walls covered in a brownish-red *lap* (a sort of pigmented concrete) was intended to be quite dark, restful to the eyes . . .

Such was the setting in which Ruhlmann, aided by a variety of lighting effects and sometimes the mysteries of backlighting, so artfully presented a vibrant collection of such a rare quality that I will not undertake to describe it. The Hôtel du Collectionneur is no more. It existed for only six months. Would that it could have been built in more durable form. Modern, but of a discreet modernism without aggressive austerity, it summarized, in its all-too-brief existence, many of the refinements of our day.

Leon Deshair
Translation by Jared Goss

Garden adjacent to the Hôtel du Collectionneur, 1925. Designed by Vacherot and Riousse. Looking toward the entrance front (top) and into a corner (bottom). Placed at the garden's center is the sculpture *L'Equilibre* (Balance) by Max Blondat.

Notes

⁜

1 "Seen in New York: Modern European Art at the Metropolitan," *Good Furniture Magazine*, vol. 22, no. 1 (January 1924), 8.

2 Thérèse Bonney and Louise Bonney. *A Shopping Guide to Paris* (New York: Robert M. McBride & Company, 1929), 169.

3 Paul Poiret. "A New Era in the Use of Color," *Arts & Decoration*, vol. 13 (October 1920), 366–7.

4 Parts of this text are adapted from previously published works by the author, including *French Art Deco* (New York: Metropolitan Museum of Art and Yale University Press, 2014) and *Art Deco Style* (New York: Assouline, 2021).

5 Léon Moussinac. *Le Meuble Français Moderne* (Paris: Librairie Hachette, 1925), 67.

6 Organized by curator Yvonne Brunhammer, *Les Années '25': Art Déco / Bauhaus / Stijl / Esprit Nouveau* was presented at the Musée des Arts Décoratifs from March 3 to May 16, 1966. Organized by curator Bevis Hillier, *Art Deco* was presented at The Minneapolis Institute of Art from July 8 to September 5, 1971.

7 United Sates Commission on International Exposition of Modern Decorative and Industrial Art, 1925, Paris, France. *Report of Commission: Appointed by the Secretary of Commerce to Visit and Report Upon the International Exposition of Modern Decorative and Industrial Art in Paris, 1925* (Washington, DC: Department of Commerce, 1925), 16.

8 The full regulations for the fair can be found in *Exposition Internationale des Arts Décoratifs et Industriels Modernes: Catalogue Générale Officiel* (Paris: Imprimerie de Vaugirard, 1925), 18–22. This English translation appears in *Report of Commission*, 17–18. See note vii above.

9 *Report of Commission*, 20. See note vii above.

10 The pavilion was funded by the French state, which took possession of its unsold furnishings at the close of the fair. Yvonne Brunhammer and Suzanne Tise. *The Decorative Arts in France: La Société des Artistes Décorateurs 1900–1942* (New York: Rizzoli, 1990), 96.

11 From the text of a lecture delivered to students at the École Boulle on June 6, 1928, 4. Courtesy of the late Florence Camard.

12 Ibid., 7.

13 Guillaume Janneau. *Technique du décor intérieur moderne* (Paris: Éditions Albert Morancé, 1927), 78.

14 Léon Moussinac. *Le Meuble Français Moderne* (Paris: Librairie Hachette, 1925), 67.

15 Marcel Zahar. "Œuvres dernières de Ruhlmann," *Art et Décoration* (January 1934), 5.

16 Ibid., 10.

17 Léon Deshairs. Preface to *L'Hôtel du Collectionneur* (Paris: Éditions Albert Lévy, 1925), 2.

18 Patout's solution was not entirely well received. In a review of the architecture of the fair, critic Georges LeFèvre compared the building to a stack of hatboxes: "Alas! If (Ruhlmann's) original and enlightened mind allowed him to create some outstanding furniture and some remarkable interiors, he was less successful in the architectural expression of his project, which is nothing more than an assembly of hatboxes that the collaboration of the Brandts, the Bernards, the Janniots, cannot save." "Exposition Internationale des Arts Décoratifs et Industriels Modernes: L'Architecture," *L'Art Vivant*, vol. 1, no. 19 (October 1, 1925), 23. Joseph Hiriart, another architect whose work was shown at the fair, was also critical: "I like less the exterior wall finishes that give this pavilion, so full of form, so harmonious in proportions, a cardboard appearance that it does not deserve." "L'Architecture," *Les Arts Décoratifs Modernes 1925* (special number of *Vient de Paraître*) (Paris: Les Éditions G. Crès et Cie, 1925), 151.

19 Henri Clouzot. "Le Pavillon du Collectionneur," *La Renaissance de L'Art Français et des Industries de Luxe*, vol. 8, no. 11 (November 1925), 528.

20 See Jacques-François Blondel, *De La Distribution des Maisons de Plaisance et de la Décoration des Edifices en general*, 1737–38. Architect-critic Joseph Hiriart noted, "This pavilion is one of the most successful at the Exposition. Inspired by Blondel. . . . Here is a happy experience that proves that one can be very modern while taking inspiration from our beautiful French past." Hiriart, 151. (See note 18 above.)

Acknowledgments

⁜

This book would not have been possible without the encouragement and support of Emmanuel Bréon and Rosalind Pepall, together with the late J. Stewart Johnson, my three esteemed co-curators on the 2004 exhibition *Ruhlmann: Genius of Art Deco*. That project marked the start of my professional interest in Ruhlmann and his Hôtel du Collectionneur.

I also owe thanks to the late Florence Camard, who shared so much of her knowledge of Ruhlmann with me.

So as not to have to reinvent the wheel, three museums generously have allowed me to adapt texts I wrote for their publications. At The Metropolitan Museum of Art, I thank Mark Polizzotti, Publisher and Editor in Chief, and Rachel High, Manager of Editorial Marketing and Rights, for allowing me to adapt material from *French Art Deco* (2014), especially "French Art Deco: An Overview" and sections addressing Ruhlmann and objects from L'Hôtel du Collectionneur; I also thank Julie Zeftel, Senior Manager of Rights and Permissions for her help with images. At the Montreal Museum of Fine Arts, I thank Sébastien Hart, Chef, Éditions Scientifiques, and at the Musée des Années 30, I thank Benjamin Couilleaux, Director, for allowing me to adapt material from the exhibition catalogue *Ruhlmann: Genius of Art Deco* (2004), especially my texts on the Hôtel du Collectionneur and objects from the pavilion.

Other institutions and individuals have been instrumental in helping with imagery, including Stéphane Asseline in Paris, Manon Leriche, Alice Aguirregabiria, and Fanny Bigeon at the Mobilier National in Paris, Marta Areia at the Museu Calouste Gulbenkian in Lisbon. At the Musée des Arts Décoratifs in Paris, I thank Anne Monier Vanryb. At *L'Illustration* magazine, I thank Jean Sébastien Baschet.

At Rizzoli, I thank my editors Philip Reeser and Ilaria Fusina for their patience, thoroughness, and support throughout the entire project. And I thank William Loccisano for the sympathetic elegance of his book design.

Image Credits

⁂

Every reasonable attempt has been made to identify owners of copyright. If the publisher is notified of errors or omissions, corrections will be made in subsequent printings or editions.

Pages 2–3 Photograph by Georges Buffotot. Musée des Arts Décoratifs, Fonds Edition Albert Lévy, inv. EAL 0-19. © Photo distr. Les Arts Décoratifs / Éditions Albert Lévy.
Page 6 Impaint / Alamy Stock Photo.
Page 8 Reprinted from Maurice Dufrène, *Ensembles Mobiliers I.* Paris: Charles Moreau, n.d (ca. 1925), plate 26. Photograph by Chevojon. Photogravure by Faucheux, Chelles.

I. French Art Deco: An Overview
Page 10 Photograph by Vincent Wulveryck. Cartier Collection © Cartier.
Page 11 The Metropolitan Museum of Art, John C. Waddell Collection. Gift of John C. Waddell, 1998 (1998.537.28). Image © The Metropolitan Museum of Art.
Pages 12 and 13 Reprinted from Henri Clouzot, "Les Arts Appliqués au Salon d'Automne" in *La Renaissance de l'Art Français et les Industries de Luxe*, vol. 8, January–December 1925, p. 5. Photographs by L. Chifflot.
Page 15 Reprinted from Jean Badovici (ed.), *Harmonies: Intérieurs de Ruhlmann*. Paris: Éditions Albert Morancé, 1924, plate 12.
Page 17 (top) Reprinted from Gabriel Mourey, *L'Art Français de la Révolution à Nos Jours*, vol. III. Paris: Librairie de France, 1922, color plate following p. 288.
Page 17 (bottom right) The Metropolitan Museum of Art. Gift of Geoffrey N. Bradfield, 1985 (1985.320.1). Image © The Metropolitan Museum of Art.
Page 17 (bottom left) Private collection. G. Dagli Orti / © NPL – DeA Picture Library / Bridgeman Images.
Pages 18–19 Thérèse Bonney. © The Regents of the University of California, The Bancroft Library, University of California, Berkeley. This work is made available under a Creative Commons Attribution 4.0 license.
Page 20 Reprinted from Michel Roux-Spitz, *Batiments et Jardins*. Paris: Éditions Albert Lévy, 1925, plate 76. Photograph by Thibaud.
Page 21 Reprinted from Jean Badovici, *Intérieurs Français*. Paris: Éditions Albert Morancé, 1925, plate 32.
Page 22 Reprinted from *Les Arts de la Maison*, vol. IV, Printemps & Été 1925. Paris: Éditions Albert Morancé 1925, plate XXXII.
Page 23 Jean Badovici, *Intérieurs Français*, plate 6.
Page 25 Reprinted from "Normandie: Le Nouveau Paquebot de la Cie. Gle. Transatlantique, Chef-d'Œuvre de la Technique et de l'Art Français," *L'Illustration*, special issue (no. 4813bis), June 1935, p. 23. (www.lillustration.com)

II. The 1925 Paris Exposition
Page 26 Heritage Image Partnership Ltd / Alamy Stock Photo.
Page 27 Michel Roux-Spitz, *Batiments et Jardins*, plate 7. Photograph by Egrez.
Page 28 (top) PWB Images / Alamy Stock Photo.
Pages 28 (bottom) and 29 (bottom) Chronicle / Alamy Stock Photo.

Page 29 (top) History and Art Collection / Alamy Stock Photo.
Pages 30–31 Reprinted from "Exposition des Arts Décoratifs," *L'Illustration*, special issue (no. 4286bis), June 1925, pp. 6–7. Watercolor by Jacques Henri Lambert. (www.lillustration.com)
Page 33 Reprinted from *La Renaissance de l'Art Français et les Industries de Luxe*, vol. 8, January–December 1925, p. 336.
Page 34 (top to bottom) Reprinted from René Chavance, *Exposition des Arts Décoratifs et Industriels Modernes, Paris 1925: Une Fête du Gout Moderne*. Paris: Éditions d'Art L. Patras, 1925, plates 4, 3, 5.
Page 35 (top) Reprinted from Henri Clouzot, "L'Exposition des Arts Décoratifs à Vol d'Oiseau" in *La Renaissance de l'Art Français et les Industries de Luxe*, vol. 8, January–December 1925, p. 203. Photograph by Paul Baron.
Page 35 (middle) Henri Clouzot, "L'Exposition des Arts Décoratifs à Vol d'Oiseau," p. 206. Photograph by G.-L. Manuel Frères.
Page 35 (bottom) Henri Clouzot, "L'Exposition des Arts Décoratifs à Vol d'Oiseau," p. 202.
Page 36 Michel Roux-Spitz, *Batiments et Jardins*, plate 2 (detail).
Page 37 (top left) Reprinted from Pierre Patout, *L'Architecture Officiel et Les Pavillons*. Paris: Éditions Charles Moreau, 1925, plate 21. Photogravure by Viale et L'Hotellier.
Page 37 (top right) Reprinted from *Mobilier et Décoration*, vol. 5, no. 8, July 1925, p. 81.
Page 37 (middle left and right) Michel Roux-Spitz, *Batiments et Jardins*, plates 21 (detail), 22. Photographs by Salaün.
Page 37 (bottom left and right) *L'Illustration* (no. 4286bis), p. 17. (www.lillustration.com)
Page 38 (top left) Michel Roux-Spitz, *Batiments et Jardins*, plate 97. Photograph by Egrez.
Page 38 (top right) Penta Springs Limited / Alamy Stock Photo.
Page 38 (middle left and middle right) *L'Illustration* (no. 4286bis), pp. 41, 37. (www.lillustration.com)
Page 38 (bottom) *L'Illustration* (no. 4286bis), p. 1. (www.lillustration.com)
Page 39 Michel Roux-Spitz, *Batiments et Jardins*, plate 62. Photograph by Thibaut.
Page 40 Michel Roux-Spitz, *Batiments et Jardins*, plate 67.
Page 41 (top left) Michel Roux-Spitz, *Batiments et Jardins*, plate 88. Photograph by Roser.
Page 41 (top right) Reprinted from *Les Arts de la Maison*, vol. V, Automne & Hiver 1925. Paris: Éditions Albert Morancé 1925, plate XXIX.
Page 41 (middle left) Michel Roux-Spitz, *Batiments et Jardins*, plate 96. Photograph by Chevojon.
Page 41 (middle right) *Les Arts de la Maison*, vol. V, Automne & Hiver 1925, plate XXXVIII.
Page 41 (bottom left) Michel Roux-Spitz, *Batiments et Jardins*, plate 83. Photograph by Reifenstein.
Page 41 (bottom right) *Les Arts de la Maison*, vol. V, Automne & Hiver 1925, plate XXII.
Page 43 (top left) *L'Illustration* (no. 4286bis), p. 2. Watercolor by Raymond Savignac. (www.lillustration.com)
Page 43 (top right) *L'Illustration* (no. 4286bis), p. 42. Watercolor by Henri Rapin. (www.lillustration.com)
Page 43 (bottom) *L'Illustration* (no.

4286bis), p. 43. Drawing by Georges Scott. (www.lillustration.com)
Page 44 (top left) *L'Illustration* (no. 4286bis), p. 40. Watercolor by Louis Bailly. (www.lillustration.com)
Page 44 (top center) Penta Springs Limited / Alamy Stock Photo.
Page 44 (top right) *L'Illustration* (no. 4286bis), p. 39. Watercolor by Henry de Renaucourt. (www.lillustration.com)
Page 44 (middle left) The Archives of the Planet / Alamy Stock Photo.
Page 44 (middle right) *L'Illustration* (no. 4286bis), p. 5. (www.lillustration.com)
Page 44 (bottom left) *L'Illustration* (no. 4286bis), p. 11. Watercolor by Henri Rapin. (www.lillustration.com)
Page 44 (bottom right) Penta Springs Limited / Alamy Stock Photo.
Page 45 Pierre Patout, *L'Architecture Officiel et Les Pavillons*, plate 29. Photogravure by Viale et L'Hotellier.
Page 46 (top left and top right) Penta Springs Limited / Alamy Stock Photo.
Page 46 (bottom left) Reprinted from Maurice Dufrène, *Ensembles Mobiliers Expostition Internationale 1925*, 2me Série. Paris: Charles Moreau, n.d. (ca. 1925), plate 21 (detail). Photogravure by Faucheux, Chelles.
Page 46 (bottom right) Michel Roux-Spitz, *Batiments et Jardins*, plate 60. Photograph by Vizzavona.
Page 47 (top left and top right) Penta Springs Limited / Alamy Stock Photo.
Page 47 (bottom left) Maurice Dufrène, *Ensembles Mobiliers Expostition Internationale 1925*, 2me Série, plate 6 (detail). Photogravure by Faucheux, Chelles.
Page 47 (bottom right) Michel Roux-Spitz, *Batiments et Jardins*, plate 53. Photograph by Salaün.
Page 48 (top left) Michel Roux-Spitz, *Batiments et Jardins*, plate 45. Photograph by Buffotot.
Page 48 (top right) Maurice Dufrène, *Ensembles Mobiliers Expostition Internationale 1925*, 2me Série, plate 29. Photogravure by Faucheux, Chelles.
Page 48 (middle left) Michel Roux-Spitz, *Batiments et Jardins*, plate 27. Photograph by Chevojon.
Page 48 (middle right) Maurice Dufrène, *Ensembles Mobiliers Expostition Internationale 1925*, 2me Série, plate 11. Photograph by Chevojon. Photogravure by Faucheux, Chelles.
Page 48 (bottom left and bottom right) Michel Roux-Spitz, *Batiments et Jardins*, plates 46 (photograph by Egrez), 47.
Page 49 *L'Illustration* (no. 4286bis), p. 35. (www.lillustration.com)

III. E. J. Ruhlmann and Pierre Patout
Page 50 © Ministère de la Culture / Médiathèque du Patrimoine, Dist. RMN Grand Palais / Art Resource, NY
Page 51 © Laure Albin Guillot / Roger-Viollet.
Page 52 (top left) Reprinted from *Pierre Patout: Architecte, Urbaniste, Décorateur*. Strasbourg: Edari, n.d. (ca. 1935), p. 15.
Page 52 (top right) Reprinted from Léon Moussinac, *Croquis de Ruhlmann*. Paris: Éditions Albert Lévy, 1924, plate 23.
Page 52 (bottom) Reprinted from *Les Arts de la Maison*, vol. 3, no. 8. Paris: Éditions Albert Morancé, 1925, p.10.
Page 53 The Metropolitan Museum of Art. Purchase, Edward C. Moore Jr. Gift, 1923 (23.174a-d). Image © The Metropolitan Museum of Art.
Page 54 Reprinted from *L'Architecte*,

vol. 8, 1913, plate LXIV.
Page 55 (top) Reprinted from "Intérieurs Modernes," *L'Illustration*. vol. 91, no. 4708, May 27, 1933, p. 47. (www.lillustration.com)
Page 55 (bottom) Jean Badovici (ed.), *Harmonies: Intérieurs de Ruhlmann*, plate 29.
Page 56 Reprinted from Henri Clouzot, "Le Miracle du Mobilier Français" in *L'Illustration*, vol. 86, no. 4452, June 30, 1928, p. 687. (www.lillustration.com)
Page 57 The Metropolitan Museum of Art. Purchase, Edward C. Moore Jr. Gift, 1925 (25.231.1). Image © The Metropolitan Museum of Art.
Page 58 (top left) Reprinted from *Jardins & Cottages*, vol. 1, no. 10, January 1927. Paris: Librairie de la Construction Moderne, p. 99.
Page 58 (top right) *Jardins & Cottages*, p. 97.
Page 58 (bottom left) *Jardins & Cottages*, p. 100.
Page 58 (bottom right) *Jardins & Cottages*, p. 102.
Page 59 Reprinted from *L'Architecte*, vol. 3, no. 4, April 1926, plate 22.
Page 60 (top left and top right) Léon Moussinac, *Croquis de Ruhlmann*, plates 3, 14.
Page 60 (bottom) Mobilier National, Paris (Inv. GME 9492). Collection of French Mobilier National. Photograph by Philippe Sébert.
Page 61 The Metropolitan Museum of Art. Purchase, Edward C. Moore Jr. Gift, 1925 (25.231.2). Image © The Metropolitan Museum of Art.
Page 62 Reprinted from R. Orgebach, "Nos Amis . . . Les Vieux Meubles dans le Décor d'Aujourd'hui" in "Intérieurs Modernes," *L'Illustration* (no. 4708), May 27, 1933, p. 43. (www.lillustration.com)
Page 63 (top, middle, bottom left, and bottom right) Jean Badovici (ed.), *Harmonies: Intérieurs de Ruhlmann*, plates 35 (detail), 33 (detail), 36, 34.
Pages 64 and 65 Henri Clouzot, "Le Miracle du Mobilier Français" in *L'Illustration*, pp. 688, 689. (www.lillustration.com)
Page 66 Photograph taken as part of the publication "On scene! Ile-de-France performance venues 1910–1940," by Julie Faure. Lieux-Dits editions, 2021. © Stephane Asseline, région Île-de-France.
Page 67 Viennaslide / Alamy Stock Photo.
Page 69 © Pascal Lemaitre. All rights reserved 2024 / Bridgeman Images.

IV. The Collector's House, 1925
Page 70 (left, center, and right) Reprinted from Leigh French Jr. and Harold Donaldson Eberlein, *The Smaller Houses and Gardens of Versailles from 1680 to 1815*. New York: The Pencil Points Press, 1926, pp. 136, 137, 138.
Page 71 Adapted from a plan by Pierre Patout as published in Antony Goissaud, "À L'Exposition des Arts Décoratifs: Le Pavillon du Collectionnneur" in *La Construction Moderne*, vol. 41, no. 14, January 3, 1926, p. 163.
Page 72 Reprinted from *La Construction Moderne*, vol. 41, no. 14, January 3, 1926, p. 157.
Page 73 *La Construction Moderne*, plate IV. Photograph by P. Cadé.
Pages 74–75 Maurice Dufrène, *Ensembles Mobiliers Expostition Internationale 1925*, 2me Série, plate 1. Photograph by Chevojon. Photogravure by Faucheux, Chelles.
Page 76 (top) Reprinted from Henri Clouzot, "Le Pavillon du

Collectionneur" in *La Renaissance de l'Art Français et les Industries de Luxe*, vol. 8, January–December 1925, p. 525. Photograph by REP.
Page 76 (bottom) Private collection. Christie's Images / Bridgeman Images.
Page 77 (top left) Fondation Glénat, Grenoble, France. © Fonds Glénat / Bridgeman Images.
Page 77 (top right) © Phillips Auctioneers Limited.
Page 77 (middle left) Museum of Fine Arts, Houston, TX. Gift of Mr. and Mrs. Meredith Long / Bridgeman Images.
Page 77 (bottom left) The Metropolitan Museum of Art. Purchase, Edward C. Moore Jr. Gift, 1925 (25.210). Image © The Metropolitan Museum of Art.
Page 77 (bottom right) The Metropolitan Museum of Art. Purchase, Edward C. Moore Jr. Gift, 1925 (25.212a, b). Image © The Metropolitan Museum of Art.
Pages 78–79 Maurice Dufrène, *Ensembles Mobiliers Expostition Internationale 1925*, 2me Série, plate 4. Photograph by Chevojon. Photogravure by Faucheux, Chelles.
Page 80 Maurice Dufrène, *Ensembles Mobiliers Expostition Internationale 1925*, 2me Série, plate 2. Photograph by Chevojon. Photogravure by Faucheux, Chelles.
Page 81 (top left) © Phillips Auctioneers Limited.
Page 81 (top right) Private collection. © NPL – DeA Picture Library / Etude Tajan / Bridgeman Images.
Page 81 (middle right, bottom left, and bottom right) Private collection. Christie's Images / Bridgeman Images.
Pages 82–83 Maurice Dufrène, *Ensembles Mobiliers Expostition Internationale 1925*, 2me Série, plate 3. Photograph by Chevojon. Photogravure by Faucheux, Chelles.
Page 84 Maurice Dufrène, *Ensembles Mobiliers Expostition Internationale 1925*, 2me Série, plate 5. Photogravure by Faucheux, Chelles.
Page 85 (top) The Metropolitan Museum of Art. Purchase, Bequest of Thelma Williams Gill, by exchange, 2002 (2002.365). Image © The Metropolitan Museum of Art.
Page 85 (middle right) The Metropolitan Museum of Art. Purchase, Edward C. Moore Jr. Gift, 1925 (25.211). Image © The Metropolitan Museum of Art.
Page 85 (bottom left) Private collection. © NPL – DeA Picture Library / Etude Tajan / Bridgeman Images.
Page 85 (bottom right) piemags / SMKM / Alamy Stock Photo.
Page 86 © Ministère de la Culture / Médiathèque du Patrimoine, Dist. RMN Grand Palais / Art Resource, NY.
Page 87 Calouste Gulbenkian Foundation, Lisbon – Calouste Gulbenkian Museum. Photograph by Catarina Gomes Ferreira.
Page 88 *La Construction Moderne*, p. 160. Photograph by Harand.

L'Hôtel du Collectionneur
Pages 89–136 Facsimile of *L'Hôtel du Collectionneur*. Paris: Éditions Albert Lévy, 1926.
Pages 137, 138 (left and right), 139 (bottom) The Archives of the Planet / Alamy Stock Photo.
Page 139 (top) and 140 (top and bottom) Penta Springs Limited / Alamy Stock Photo.

– 143 –

First published in
the United States of America in 2025 by
Rizzoli Electa, a division of
Rizzoli International Publications, Inc.
49 West 27th Street
New York, New York 10001
www.rizzoliusa.com

PUBLISHER: Charles Miers
ASSOCIATE PUBLISHER: Margaret Chace
EDITORS: Ilaria Fusina Woodward and Philip Reeser
PRODUCTION MANAGER: Alyn Evans
DESIGN COORDINATOR: Tim Biddick
COPY EDITOR: Claudia Bauer
MANAGING EDITOR: Lynn Scrabis

DESIGNER: William Loccisano

Copyright © 2025 by Jared Goss

BOOK, FRONT COVER: Grand salon, the Hôtel du Collectionneur

BOOK, BACK COVER: Dining room, the Hôtel du Collectionneur

SLIPCASE, FRONT COVER: Grand salon, the Hôtel du Collectionneur

SLIPCASE, BACK COVER: Garden façade, the Hôtel du Collectionneur

ENDPAPERS: Adapted by William Loccisano from a design by Henri Stephany.
A silk textile in this pattern covered the walls of the grand salon of the Hôtel du Collectionneur.

PAGES 2–3: The Hôtel du Collectionneur by night, 1925.
Visible on the two covered porches are fresco paintings by Henri Marret.
Above the windows is a bas-relief by Joseph Bernard.
In front of the building is a sculpture by Alfred Janniot.

PAGE 6: Poster for the 1925 Paris Exposition. Designed by Robert Bonfils.

All rights reserved.
No part of this publication may be reproduced, stored in a retrieval system,
or transmitted in any form or by any means, electronic, mechanical, photocopying, recording,
or otherwise, without prior consent of the publishers.

ISBN: 978-0-8478-7435-4
Library of Congress Control Number: 2025931528

Printed in Italy
2025 2026 2027 2028 / 10 9 8 7 6 5 4 3 2 1

The authorized representative in the EU for product safety
and compliance is
Mondadori Libri S.p.A.
via Gian Battista Vico, 42
20123 Milan
Italy
www.mondadori.it